Collins

11+
Maths Arithmetic & Word Problems

Support & Practice Workbook

Chris Pearse and Jessica Hodge

Published by Collins
An imprint of HarperCollins*Publishers* Ltd
1 London Bridge Street
London SE1 9GF

HarperCollins*Publishers*
Macken House
39/40 Mayor Street Upper
Dublin 1
D01 C9W8
Ireland

ISBN 978-0-00-849742-2

First published 2021

10 9 8 7 6 5 4 3 2 1

British Library Cataloguing in Publication Data.
A CIP record of this book is available from the British Library.
Publisher: Clare Souza
Authors: Chris Pearse and Jessica Hodge
Project Management: Richard Toms and Sundus Pasha
Cover Design: Kevin Robbins and Sarah Duxbury
Inside Concept Design: Ian Wrigley
Typesetting and artwork: Jouve India Private Limited
Production: Karen Nulty

Published in collaboration with Teachitright.
Billy the Bookworm™ is the property of Teachitright Ltd.

Printed in the United Kingdom.

Contents

Contents

Introduction

Teachitright

This book has been published in collaboration with Teachitright, one of the most successful 11+ tuition companies in the South-East. It has supported thousands of children for both grammar school and independent school entry. Teachitright has several tuition centres across the UK, including Berkshire, Buckinghamshire, Surrey and the West Midlands.

With considerable experience and knowledge, Teachitright has produced a range of books to support children through their 11+ journey for both CEM style and many Common Entrance exams. The books have been written by qualified teachers, tested in the classroom with pupils and adapted to ensure children are fully prepared and able to perform to the best of their ability.

Teachitright's unique mascot, Billy the Bookworm, helps to guide children through this book and gives helpful hints and tips along the way. We hope your child finds this book useful and informative and we wish them luck on their 11+ journey.

Teachitright hold a number of comprehensive revision courses and mock exams throughout the year. For more information, visit **www.teachitright.com**

Helping to build your child's future

This Maths Arithmetic and Word Problems Support and Practice Workbook provides the perfect preparation for both 11+ and Common Entrance exams. It covers these key topics:

- Working with numbers

- Equivalent numbers

- Algebraic calculations

- Statistics

- Data handling and interpretation

- Shape and space

How to Use this Book

As this book is broken down into lessons that cover different topics, it can be used to focus on individual areas of development or to work through every mathematical topic.

Learn: An informative teaching section to help with the key points and techniques for that lesson topic. It includes worked examples.

Develop: An opportunity to practise short calculations based on the lesson topic to ensure key principles and techniques are fully understood.

Timed tests: Strategically placed, progressive timed tests to help build confidence with worded problems and time management.

The answer section gives detailed explanations to aid revision. There is also a glossary on page 132. It is important for the child to understand and learn key words and phrases that are likely to appear in the exam.

At the back of the book, a **marking chart** and **progress grid** help to track your child's development throughout the topics and highlight strengths and weaknesses.

Online Video Tutorial

An online video tutorial to help with techniques is available at www.collins.co.uk/11plusresources

SECTION 1:

WORKING WITH NUMBERS

Look out for Billy's tips and hints.

LEARN

Place value is a key element to all mathematics. In this first lesson you will grasp the main principles involved in understanding the value of a digit in a number. The value of a digit is determined by its place in relation to the position of the decimal point.

For example:

In Oliver's bank account he has £3465.00. The value of 3 is £3000, the value of 4 is £400 and the value of 6 is £60.

In Hannah's bank account she has £346.50 and the value of 3 is £300.

In Alice's bank account she has £34.65 and the value of 3 is £30.

The table below demonstrates the value of each digit.

3	2	1	5	6	7	8	9	1	.	2	3	5	4	8	1
THREE HUNDRED MILLION	TWENTY MILLION	ONE MILLION	FIVE HUNDRED THOUSAND	SIXTY THOUSAND	SEVEN THOUSAND	EIGHTH HUNDRED	NINETY	ONE		TWO TENTHS	THREE HUNDREDTHS	FIVE THOUSANDTHS	FOUR TEN THOUSANDTHS	EIGHT HUNDRED THOUSANDTHS	ONE MILLIONTH

It is important to understand the value of decimals (that is, the digits written to the right of the decimal point).

For example: 3.476

4 is written one place to the right of the decimal point; so it has been divided by 10 or could be written as $\frac{4}{10}$ or 0.4

7 is written two places to the right of the decimal point; so it has been divided by 100 or could be written as $\frac{7}{100}$ or 0.07

6 is written three places to the right of the decimal point; so it has been divided by 1000 or could be written as $\frac{6}{1000}$ or 0.006

DEVELOP

① Using the number below, answer the following questions:

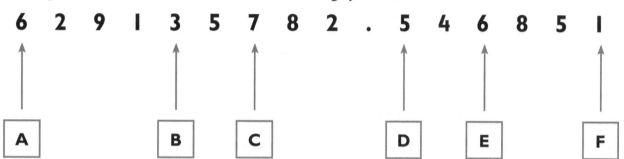

Write the value of the digits at:

A =

B =

C =

D =

E =

F =

② Place a decimal point in the numbers below so that the number has:

a)   2 tens in it

    i)   3 6 2 1 4 3

    ii)   7 2 8 9 1

b)   3 tenths in it

    i)   4 6 2 3 8

    ii)   2 3 9 4 1

Lesson 2: Rounding Numbers

LEARN

Rounding is when you write a number that isn't exact but you retain its **approximate values**. For example, 41 rounded to the nearest ten is 40. You may be asked to round (or rewrite) a number to the nearest ten, hundred, or thousand, or tenth, hundredth or thousandth. You may also be asked to round to one, two or three **decimal places** or to a number of **significant figures (SF)**. This lesson demonstrates how this is done.

Example one: Round 6825.9341 to the nearest thousand

Let's take you through the steps you need to make.

①   Identify the relevant digit and underline it.   **<u>6</u>845.9351**

②   Look to the right of that relevant digit and, if it is followed by a number which is 5 or more, you must round up. As it is followed by the digit 8, you must round up to the next thousand.

       The rounded number is now 7000.

Example two: Rewrite 6845.9351 to the nearest tenth

Take the steps given in example one.

①   The relevant number is 9 tenths.   **6845.<u>9</u>351**

②   9 is followed by a 3 so as 3 is less than 5 you do not round up, therefore it remains 9 tenths.

The rounded number to the nearest tenth is now 6845.9

Example three: Round 6845.9351 to two decimal places

①   The digit in the second decimal place is 3   **6845.9<u>3</u>51**

②   3 is followed by 5 so 3 is rounded up.

       The rounded number is now 6845.94

Example four: Round 6845.9351 to two significant figures

Significant figures are used when we want a rough idea of a number or an approximation.

①   To round 6845.9351 to two significant figures, find the two most important numbers. The first most important number is 6 because it tells us the number is six thousand and something.

②   The second most significant number is 8. Remember to round up or down where required as in previous examples.

       The number to two significant figures (SF) is 6800.

DEVELOP

Try these rounding questions.

① Rewrite 86 734.287 to the nearest:

    a)   hundred

    b)   hundredth

    c)   ten

    d)   tenth

② Rewrite 2864.37 to:

    a)   one decimal place

    b)   one significant figure

    c)   two significant figures

③ Round 867.429 to the nearest:

    a)   whole number

    b)   two decimal places

    c)   three significant figures

5 or more, let it soar.

4 or less, let it rest.

TIMED TEST 1

Circle the letter above the correct answer with a pencil.

① What is the correct value of the underlined digit? 2<u>3</u>5 721.864

A	B	C	D	E
300	30	$\frac{3}{100}$	30 000	300 000

② Help Nishaan to place a decimal point in the following number so that '4' has a value of four hundred: 6 294 165 782

A	B	C	D	E
62.94165782	629 416.5782	62 941.65782	6294.165782	6.294165782

③ Alice was asked to select the biggest number in a maths quiz. Which should she select?

A	B	C	D	E
3678.9	3.6789	36.789	367.89	0.36789

④ What is the value of the underlined digit? 83.64<u>2</u>1

A	B	C	D	E
twenty	two	two thousand	two hundredths	two thousandths

⑤ Manreet was lent some money. She was asked to pay it back to the nearest ten pounds. £29 452.95 was loaned to her. How much should she pay back?

A	B	C	D	E
£29 000.95	£29 400	£29 450	£29 452.90	£30 000

⑥ The total number of people who attended a rock festival was 128 468. What is this rounded to two significant figures?

A	B	C	D	E
100 500	108 000	100 008	120 000	130 000

⑦ A range of mountain heights was given in a geography lesson. The children were asked to select the highest peak. Which height should they choose?

A	B	C	D	E
23 402 ft	23 042 ft	23 420 ft	23 024 ft	23 204 ft

⑧ The fastest lap time in a motor race was 83.356 seconds. What is this time to three significant figures?

A	B	C	D	E
83.4 s	80.35 s	83.3 s	80.305 s	83.006 s

⑨ A box contains 48 tins of nails. Estimate the total number of tins in 731 boxes.

A	B	C	D	E
350	3500	35 000	2800	28 000

⑩ Hannah was asked to research the Roman town of Colchester for a school project. The total population in 2014 was 186 493. To help draw a line graph, she rounded the population to the nearest hundred. What was the rounded number?

A	B	C	D	E
186 400	187 490	186 000	186 500	190 000

⑪ A factory produced 12 356 cars in a month. What is this number to the nearest 10 000?

A	B	C	D	E
10 000	12 000	110 000	14 000	13 000

⑫ A shop sold 13 963 shoes in a week. How many is this to the nearest 100?

A	B	C	D	E
13 900	14 000	13 000	13 600	14 900

⑬ Oliver's student union, at university, in total collected 3 456 209 kg of rubbish in a year. How much is this to the nearest hundred thousand?

A	B	C	D	E
3 456 200 kg	3 456 000 kg	3 450 000 kg	3 500 200 kg	3 500 000 kg

⑭ Jovan was asked to write the number six hundred and five million five thousand and twenty-seven. He got the number correct. Which number did he write?

A	B	C	D	E
605 005 027	650 050 027	655 027	60 005 527	605 050 027

⑮ Jasveer is doing a sponsored drumming challenge and has to play his drums constantly for as long as possible. He plays for 1 hour 27 minutes and 32.478 seconds. What is his time to the nearest tenth of a second?

A	B	C	D	E
1 h 27 m 23.4 s	1 h 27 m 20 s	1 h 30 m 32.480 s	1 h 27 m 30 s	1 h 27 m 32.5 s

Lesson 3: Special Numbers and Number Sequences

LEARN

It is always useful to be able to recognise 'special' numbers. Included here are **prime numbers, square numbers, cube numbers** and **triangular numbers** as well as **odd numbers, even numbers** and **multiples**.

Many number sequences (a list of numbers) are made up of these 'special' numbers, so time could be saved very effectively by recognising, in both ascending and descending order, the number sequences.

PRIME NUMBERS: A prime number is a number with only two **factors**, itself and number 1. The smallest prime number is 2, which is the only even number to be prime.

Here are the first 15 terms in the prime number sequence:

2, 3, 5, 7, 11, 13, 17, 19, 23, 29, 31, 37, 41, 43, 47

SQUARE NUMBERS: A square number is a number that results from a number being multiplied by itself. In other words, the square number results from raising another number to the power of 2.

For example:
The square number refers to the number of dots which are arranged in a square pattern. This can be shown below:

1×1 2×2 3×3 4×4 5×5

3 squared (or 3^2) = 3 × 3 = 9   so 9 is the square number.

Here are the first 15 terms in the square number sequence:

1, 4, 9, 16, 25, 36, 49, 64, 81, 100, 121, 144, 169, 196, 225

LEARN

CUBE NUMBERS: A cube number results from multiplying a number by itself and by itself again. In other words, the cube number results from raising another number to the power of 3.

For example:

2 cubed (or 2^3) is 2 × 2 × 2 = 8, so 8 is the cube number.

4 cubed (or 4^3) is 4 × 4 × 4 = 64, so 64 is the cube number.

Here are the first 15 terms in the cube number sequence:

1, 8, 27, 64, 125, 216, 343, 512, 729, 1000, 1331, 1728, 2197, 2744, 3375

TRIANGULAR NUMBERS: Like square numbers which can be illustrated in a square pattern, you can illustrate triangular numbers in two types of triangle patterns.

Whichever way you arrange the dots, they make the same number sequence.

| 1 | 3 | 6 | 10 | 15 | | 1 | 3 | 6 | 10 | 15 |

Here are the first 15 terms in the triangular number sequence:

1, 3, 6, 10, 15, 21, 28, 36, 45, 55, 66, 78, 91, 105, 120

Each time the difference in the terms goes up by 1.

For example:

1 + 2 = 3

3 + 3 = 6

6 + 4 = 10

Other types of 'special' numbers could include odd numbers, even numbers and multiples.

LEARN

When you are given a number sequence, the first thing you should do is look to see whether you can recognise any of the 'special' numbers. If you cannot recognise the numbers as 'special', then calculate the difference between each number. You may then notice a pattern.

Example one:
6, 11, 16, 21, 26, 31

There is a '+ 5' difference between each number.

Example two:
3, 5, 6, 10, 9, 15, 12, 20, 15, 25, 18

This is called an alternate sequence because you can recognise multiples of 3 alternating with multiples of 5. Such sequences are often identified by their length: they are normally of longer length (that is, they have more terms) and the consecutive terms may increase and then decrease in value.

Example three:
0, 1, 1, 2, 3, 5, 8, 13, 21, 34

A Fibonacci sequence is also important to recognise. This is when the previous two numbers have been added together to make the next number in the sequence, e.g. 0 + 1 = 1, 1 + 1 = 2, 1 + 2 = 3, 2 + 3 = 5, etc.

The numbers in a number sequence are called 'terms'.

DEVELOP

Fill in the three missing terms in each given sequence.

1. 16, 25, 36, 49, 64, ____, ____, ____

2. 7, 11, 13, 17, 19, ____, ____, ____

3. 225, 196, 169, 144, 121, ____, ____, ____

4. 1, ____ 27, ____ 125, ____

5. 8, 6, 16, 12, 24, 18, 32, ____, ____, ____

6. 1, 3, ____ 10, 15, ____ 28, ____

7. 81, 72, ____ 54, ____ 36, ____

8. 1, 1, 2, 3, 5, 8, ____, ____, ____

9. 4, 9, 19, 39, 79, ____, ____, ____

10. 960, 480, ____ 120, ____ 30, ____

Note down the differences between the sequences to help work out the link, for example: 2, (+2) 4, (+2) 6.

Lesson 4: Addition and Subtraction

LEARN

Introduction to the four maths operations

There are four main operations in maths. Like place value, their understanding is the foundation to all maths and calculations generally.

The operations are **addition, subtraction, multiplication** and **division**.

In order to understand and select what operation is being asked for, it is important that you are able to recognise the vocabulary used. The table below lists the common vocabulary associated with each operation:

ADDITION	SUBTRACTION	MULTIPLICATION	DIVISION
Add	Subtract	Times	Divide
More	Take away	Multiply	Share among
Greater than	Leave	Groups of	Share equally
Increase	Decrease	Lots of	Fractions of
Plus	Less	Product	Equal groups
Altogether	Take	Double	Quotient
Sum	Difference	Square	
Total	Change	Cube	
Perimeter	From	Area	
	Fewer	Volume	
	Reduce by		

Once you have recognised what operation the question is asking you to use, it is important that you select the most appropriate technique so that you can be accurate and also save time. Do not rely on mental arithmetic as this can often lead to mistakes.

In this lesson we will look at both addition and subtraction.

LEARN

Let's look at addition first, where you add numbers together. The column technique is probably the most effective and quickest method to use.

Example one: Simple addition

What is 2389 and 467 added together?

Step 1: Put the larger number on top.

Step 2: Keep the digits in their appropriate place value column.

Step 3: Don't forget to regroup.

$$
\begin{array}{r}
2389\,+ \\
467 \\
\hline
2856 \\
\end{array}
$$
$_{1\ 1}$

Example two: Addition with a decimal point

What is 928.460 added to 37.923?

Follow steps 1 to 3 above.

$$
\begin{array}{r}
928.460\,+ \\
37.923 \\
\hline
966.383 \\
\end{array}
$$
$_{1\ 1}$

Step 4: If you have been asked to add decimals, don't forget to line up the decimal points.

Regrouping is often used in subtraction and addition. It is also known as 'carrying' and 'borrowing' numbers.

LEARN

In subtraction, the column technique will also be the most appropriate for saving time.

Remember to read the question very carefully in order to be able to work out which number needs to be subtracted. If you don't have enough value in the units column, you must **exchange** (borrow) and **regroup**.

Example three: Simple subtraction

What is the difference between 605 and 428?

This is where you can exchange and regroup. This is how you can do it:

In the units column, 5 is less than 8 so you will need to exchange with the column next to it before starting the subtraction. Since there are no tens, you must borrow 10 tens from the hundreds column. Next, you must take 1 from the tens column, leaving 9 tens and place it in the units column to give you 15.

$$605 -$$
$$428$$
$$\overline{}$$

Now you are ready to do the subtraction.

The final answer is 177. You can check whether this is the correct answer using the inverse, by adding 177 to 428. When added together they make 605.

$$\overset{5\ 9}{6}\,\cancel{0}\,\overset{}{}5 -$$
$$428$$
$$\overline{177}$$

Please be careful. Many questions are written and designed to be confusing and awkward in their wording. Take a few seconds to recognise the vocabulary and understand what the question is actually asking you to do.

DEVELOP

Try these addition and subtraction questions.

① What is 95.6 more than 257.52?

② Decrease 58.6 by 39.71

③ Find the sum of 259.6 and 867.83

④ Take 78.95 from 100.28

⑤ Increase 987.4 by 25.6

⑥ Take 0.8 from 80

⑦ Find the difference between 0.007 and 7

⑧ What is the sum of 2098.91 and 879.092?

⑨ What change from £1000 do I get if I spend £263.45?

⑩ Add together 9.85, 98.5 and 985

Take care when placing your decimal point into your answer.

TIMED TEST 2

① In one football season at school, the Year 5 children score a total of 142 goals and the Year 6 children score a total of 168. How many goals are scored altogether?

A	**B**	**C**	**D**	**E**
300	301	310	320	315

② A swimming pool contains 6000 litres of water. If 3214 litres are pumped out to lower the water level, how many litres are left?

A	**B**	**C**	**D**	**E**
2678 L	2786 L	2876 L	2688 L	3686 L

③ Claire has a vegetable garden. It is 9.75 m long. She increases the length by 2.8 m. How long is Claire's garden now?

A	**B**	**C**	**D**	**E**
12.55 m	15.25 m	15.15 m	18.25 m	12.25 m

④ Sam puts four lengths of wood together. One is 87.91 cm, one is 36.32 cm, one is 209.40 cm and one is 8.06 cm. What is the total sum of their lengths?

A	**B**	**C**	**D**	**E**
346.19 cm	463.19 cm	431.69 cm	369.46 cm	341.69 cm

⑤ On Monday, Emma cycles 4 km. On Wednesday, she cycles 1.25 km less than on the Monday. How many metres does Emma cycle on Wednesday?

A	**B**	**C**	**D**	**E**
2057 m	2570 m	5250 m	2750 m	5270 m

⑥ In maths, Jovan was asked to find the difference in length between two pieces of rope. One was 0.089 m and the other was 8.9 m. What was the difference?

A	**B**	**C**	**D**	**E**
8.811 m	8.181 m	8.118 m	1.881 m	8.188 m

⑦ Felicity runs the London Marathon, which is 42.2 km long. She runs for 31.5 km and she walks for 6.9 km before her final run to the finish. How long is Felicity's final run?

A	**B**	**C**	**D**	**E**
4.2 km	3.8 km	8.3 km	3.2 km	8.4 km

⑧ My teacher, Mr Dolamore, went on a diet. In month one, he lost 2.5 kg, in month two he lost 1.75 kg and in month three he lost 2.25 kg. In month four, he decided to treat himself and gained 0.66 kg. How many kilograms did Mr Dolamore lose altogether?

A	B	C	D	E
4.85 kg	8.54 kg	5.48 kg	5.49 kg	5.84 kg

⑨ The maximum weight allowed in the school lift is 350 kg. Four teachers are in the lift, weighing 62.5 kg, 60.32 kg, 80 kg and 83.3 kg. If one more person wants to get in the lift, what is the maximum weight they can be?

A	B	C	D	E
88.66 kg	86.86 kg	66.88 kg	68.86 kg	63.88 kg

⑩ Pinak runs 7.7 km on Monday, 12.3 km on Tuesday and 9.5 km on Wednesday. How far does Pinak run altogether?

A	B	C	D	E
30.5 km	25.9 km	28.6 km	29.5 km	29.05 km

⑪ Paris goes to various clubs during the week. Every Friday she attends a maths club for one hour. On Monday she goes to gym for one and a half hours, on Tuesday she attends ice skating for one and three quarter hours, and on Thursday she is at athletics club for three and a quarter hours. What is the total number of hours that Paris spends at clubs in a week?

A	B	C	D	E
6.5 h	5.7 h	7.5 h	7.25 h	5.5 h

⑫ Hafsah was asked in her mental maths test to calculate taking a hundred metres from ten thousand metres. She answered it correctly. What was her answer?

A	B	C	D	E
9000 m	9900 m	8900 m	9190 m	9090 m

⑬ Billy had to select 38 photographs from his collection of 201 for an exhibition in his village art festival. How many photographs did he have left?

A	B	C	D	E
153	167	163	165	162

⑭ Ali is asked how many sides there are in three pentagons, two rectangles, two scalene triangles, three isosceles triangles and seven octagons. What is the answer?

A	B	C	D	E
84	89	91	94	86

⑮ Neil had to deliver Easter eggs to friends and family. His first journey was 12.4 miles, the second was 43.9 miles, the third was 0.6 miles, the fourth was 28.8 miles and the final journey was 19.7 miles. How far in miles did Neil travel in total?

A	B	C	D	E
150.4	105.4	140.5	104.5	154.5

Lesson 5: Multiplication

LEARN

To help you multiply, it is important that you know your **times tables**. You should also **estimate** the answers before applying a method to help decide what your answer should roughly look like. This lesson will provide methods to help you solve complex multiplication questions.

Example one: A decimal number multiplied by an integer

6.4×3

You can estimate this by calculating $6 \times 3 = 18$

You know it will be more than 18 as 6.4 is bigger than 6. The actual answer is 19.2

Once you have estimated your answer, you can start your calculation. The formal multiplication technique will be used.

First calculate it without the decimal point.

$$
\begin{array}{r}
6\,4 \times \\
3 \\
\hline
 \\
\hline
\end{array}
\qquad
\begin{array}{r}
6\,4 \times \\
3 \\
\hline
2 \\
\hline
\scriptstyle 1 \\
\end{array}
\qquad
\begin{array}{r}
6\,4 \times \\
3 \\
\hline
1\,9\,2 \\
\hline
\scriptstyle 1 \\
\end{array}
$$

Coding 1

The order of multiplication is:

$$
\begin{array}{l}
A\,B \times \\
C \\
\hline
 \\
\hline
\end{array}
\qquad
\begin{array}{l}
C \times B \\
C \times A
\end{array}
$$

It's important to follow the right order when multiplying to get the correct answer.

LEARN

Once you have the digits in place, you must accurately place the decimal point into the answer.

Here is a system to help you:

KEY   _   = digit

       .   = decimal point

$\_ \cdot \ominus \times$	$\_ \cdot \_ \times$	$6 . 4 \times$
$\_$	$\_$	3
$\overline{}$	$\overline{}$	$\overline{}$
$\_\ \_\ \_$	$\_\ \_ \cdot \ominus$	$19 . ②$

Step 1:

Add in the decimal point from the question and see how many digits are to the right of it. In this example there is only one.

Step 2:

In the answer circle one digit from the right, and place the decimal point to the left of it.

The answer is 19.2

Example two: Two decimal numbers multiplied together

8.2×4.9

You can estimate this by calculating $8 \times 5 = 40$. The actual answer is 40.18

By referring to Coding 1, you can expand it and use Coding 2 to help you with the order of multiplication:

Coding 2

A B ×	C × B	First row (△)
C D	C × A	
0 △	D × B	Second row (▲)
▲	D × A	

LEARN

Step 1: It is important that you place a zero into the calculation to represent a ten, to indicate that you are multiplying by the 'ten' digit.

Step 2: Along the same line as the zero you multiply everything by 4 (or 40).

Step 3: Then multiply all the digits by 9 in the same order and place the products in the row below.

```
     82 ×
     49
  ───────
   3280
    738
  ───────
      |
```

Step 4: Once the multiplication is complete, you have to add up the two rows.

```
     82 ×
     49
  ───────
   3280 +
    738
  ───────
   4018
  ───────
    |  |
```

Step 5: You now have to accurately place the decimal point.

Once the decimal point has been added in the calculation, you will see there are two digits to the right of it so there will be two digits to the right of a decimal point in the answer.

```
  _ · ⊝ ×          _ · _ ×
  _ · ⊝            _ · _
  ───────          ───────
      0                0
  ───────          ───────
  _ _ _ _          _ _ · ⊝⊝
```

```
   8 .② ×
   4 .⑨
  ───────
   3280
    738
  ───────
  40.①⑧
```

Therefore, your answer is 40.18

LEARN

Example three: Two-digit number multiplied by a three-digit number

215 × 75

You can estimate this by calculating 200 × 80 = 16 000. The actual answer is 16 125.

Follow the steps taken in Example two.

```
  2 1 5 ×
    7 5
─────────
      0
─────────

─────────
```

By referring to Coding 2 and expanding it, you can use Coding 3 to help you with the order of multiplication:

Coding 3

```
  A B C ×
    D E
─────────
      0  (△)
         (▲)
─────────
```

The order of multiplication is:

D × C
D × B } First row △
D × A

E × C
E × B } Second row ▲
E × A

You can now calculate Example 3 by following the Coding 3 order.

```
  2 1 5 ×        7 × 5 = 35
    7 5          7 × 1 =  7
─────────        7 × 2 = 14
1 5 0 5 0
  1 3
─────────        5 × 5 = 25
                 5 × 1 =  5
─────────        5 × 2 = 10
```

LEARN

Then add up what has been calculated:

```
    2 1 5 ×
      7 5
  ─────────
1 5 0 5 0 +
  1 0 7 5
  ─────────
1 6 1 2 5
      │
```

So the answer to 215 × 75 = 16 125

If the question has a decimal, as in the example below, you can calculate the answer using the same steps:

Step 1: Circle the digits to the right of the decimal point.

```
  − · ⊖ ⊖
    − · ⊖
  ─────────

  ─────────
− − · ⊖⊖⊖
  ─────────
```

Step 2: As there are three digits to the right of the decimal point, there will be three digits to the right in the answer. Your answer is 16.125 (your estimate was 16).

```
    2 . ①⑤ ×
      7⑤
  ─────────
1 5 0 5 0 +
  1 0 7 5
  ─────────
1 6 . ①②⑤
```

DEVELOP

Try these multiplication questions.

①   Multiply 20 by 30

②   Find the product of 300 and 90

③   Calculate 6 lots of 0.8

④   Work out 0.4 mm times 0.6 mm

⑤   Double 28.4

⑥   Multiply 8 and 865.4

⑦   Find the product of 28.64 and 3.2

⑧   Times together 8.3 and 6.7

⑨   Work out 34 lots of £19.75

⑩   What is the total of 89 groups of 2.68?

Place the zero in automatically so you don't forget it or your answer will be incorrect.

TIMED TEST 3

15:00
15 minutes

① There are 324 beech trees in a forest. There are six times as many oak trees. How many oak trees are there?

A	B	C	D	E
54	9141	972	1944	1494

② The drama class performed their play 14 times. The average audience for each show was 286. How many people watched their performance altogether?

A	B	C	D	E
4004	4404	4440	300	3000

③ Alice buys 86 special stamps for her collection. Each costs £4.75. How much does Alice pay altogether?

A	B	C	D	E
£405.80	£408.50	£458.50	£485.50	£548.50

④ Myra asks John to build a book shelf for 32 photo albums. Each album is 46.5 mm wide. If all the albums were stacked tightly together, what is the minimum width of shelf that John would need to build?

A	B	C	D	E
1884 mm	8184 mm	4818 mm	1848 mm	1488 mm

⑤ A boat carries a total of 23 passengers on each trip from Brightlingsea to Mersea Island. It can do a maximum of 146 trips a day in July. What is the maximum number of passengers the boat could transport in one day in July?

A	B	C	D	E
3358	3538	3853	3385	3583

⑥ A school cook orders 324 packets of napkins. There are 45 napkins in each packet. How many individual napkins are ordered altogether?

A	B	C	D	E
15480	15850	14580	14850	18450

⑦ A school orders 64 maths books. There are 326 pages in each book. How many pages are there altogether?

A	B	C	D	E
20488	20468	20846	20864	20684

⑧ Ben celebrated finishing his exams by going on holiday with his two best friends. He went for 18 nights, staying at a bed and breakfast for £21.50 a night per person. What was the total bill for Ben and his friends?

A	B	C	D	E
£1261	£1611	£1161	£1160	£1116

⑨ Jasveer has a total of 32 pets. On average, it costs £0.67 per pet, per day, to feed. What is the total cost in August to feed his pets?

A	B	C	D	E
£992.87	£664.64	£644.66	£666.44	£99.20

⑩ Naomi wrote an essay. The average number of words per line on a page was 19, and there were 34 lines on a page. She wrote 8 pages in total. What was the total number of words in her essay?

A	B	C	D	E
5618	5861	5668	6581	5168

⑪ Paula helped to knit a set of nativity characters. For each wise man she knitted, on average, 43 stitches per row and 216 rows. She knitted three wise men. How many stitches altogether did she knit?

A	B	C	D	E
26864	26487	27864	27648	27468

⑫ Brian's football team won a tournament. Six teams in total took part. Each team played each other in the first round, then the two teams with the most points played in the final. If each game of football lasted 6 minutes each half, how many minutes of football did Brian's team play?

A	B	C	D	E
72	84	42	96	48

⑬ A football club hired 253 coaches to take supporters to a cup final. On average, each coach carried 84 passengers. What was the total number of passengers transported?

A	B	C	D	E
22251	25221	22252	21252	22512

⑭ It costs Finlay an average of £1.09 per litre of petrol. It takes 42 litres to completely fill the fuel tank of his car. To make a return trip to Bristol, he needs to completely fill his tank three times. How much does it cost Finlay in petrol?

A	B	C	D	E
£137.34	£45.78	£126.00	£91.56	£134.73

⑮ Olivia has to order enough pens for her school for the following term. She needs to buy five boxes per year group. There are six year groups and 50 packets in a box. Each packet costs £5.50. What is the total price of the order?

A	B	C	D	E
£8520	£8250	£8205	£1650	£1500

Lesson 6: Division

LEARN

Division is the **inverse** of multiplication and therefore it is important to know your times tables and to estimate when answering.

For example: 84 divided by 42

You know that 80 divided by 40 is 2 (8 divided by 4 is 2).

Throughout this division section you will be doing the **short division technique**. This is often known as the 'bus stop' method. The chunking method can be used but normally it is a far slower technique.

Example one: Dividing into a three-digit number

726 ÷ 3

In order for you to answer this, you will need to take the following steps.

Step 1: Lay out the calculation into the 'bus shelter'.

$$3\overline{)726}$$

Step 2: How many 3s go into the first digit of 7 (although you know it is in fact 700)? The answer is 2 with a remainder of 1.

$$3\overline{)7^12\,6}$$
2

Step 3: How many 3s go into 12? The answer is 4.

$$3\overline{)7^12\,6}$$
24

Step 4: How many 3s go into 6? The answer is 2.

$$3\overline{)7^12\,6}$$
242

The answer to 726 divided by 3 is 242.

LEARN

Example two: Dividing into a five-digit number

What is the quotient of 15 618 and 6?

Follow the above steps by working along the 'bus shelter' layout.

```
6 | 1 5 6 1 8
```

```
    0
6 | 1 5 6 1 8
```

```
    0 2
6 | 1 ¹5 6 1 8
```

```
    0 2 6
6 | 1 ¹5³6 1 8
```

```
      0 2 6 0
6 | 1 ¹5³6 1 8
```

```
      0 2 6 0 3
6 | 1 ¹5³6 1 ⁰8
```

> The question in Example two can also be written as what is $\frac{1}{6}$ of 15 618? It is the same as saying divided by 6.

The answer to the quotient of 15 618 and 6 is 2603.

LEARN

Example three: Division and fractions

What is $\frac{5}{6}$ of 15 618?

First you divide by the denominator (bottom number), which is 6. Then you times the quotient by the numerator (top number).

$$\frac{0\,2\,6\,0\,3}{6\,\overline{\smash{)}\,1\,^15\,^36\,1\,^18}} \times 5 = 1\,3\,0\,1\,5$$

Example four: Long division technique

What is 4389 divided by 19?

As you are asked to divide by a number that is more than one digit (19), you will be using the long division technique. Calculate as if you are using the short division technique but work out the remainders below the bus shelter, forming a 'long shape' calculation.

This is shown below:

a) $19\overline{)4389}$

b) $19\overline{)4389}$ remainder 0

c) $19\overline{)4389}$ giving 02, 38, 058

d) $19\overline{)4389}$ giving 0231
$38\downarrow$
058
$57\downarrow$
019
19
00
$= 231$

4389 divided by 19 = 231

DEVELOP

Have a go at the following questions.

①   Divide 175 by 5

②   What is $\frac{1}{2}$ of 5678?

③   What is $\frac{3}{5}$ of 51 025?

④   What is the quotient of 82 104 and 24?

⑤   Share 5544 among 24

⑥   How many 30s go into 4260?

⑦   What is 3744 divided by 16?

⑧   What is the quotient of 15 408 and 48?

⑨   What is $\frac{2}{3}$ of 720?

⑩   Divide 11 802 by 21

TIMED TEST 4

15:00 15 minutes

① Jessica buys eight pencils for 96 p. What is the cost of one pencil?

A	**B**	**C**	**D**	**E**
15 p	12 p	£7.68	16 p	13 p

② Sophia spends £6 on 24 large oranges. What is the cost of one orange?

A	**B**	**C**	**D**	**E**
£0.24	£1.44	£2.50	£0.25	£0.40

③ The school canteen makes 540 ham rolls every day. One packet of ham makes 15 rolls. How many packets of ham does the canteen need to purchase for each day?

A	**B**	**C**	**D**	**E**
8100	32	360	320	36

④ Members of Ava's class have been challenged to gain as many merit marks as they can. A special award will be given to anyone gaining 400 merit marks. Ava estimates she can get 16 merit marks a week. How many weeks will it take Ava to get 400 merit marks?

A	**B**	**C**	**D**	**E**
64	46	52	25	40

⑤ Peter is asked to organise a school trip for 255 students. 17 teachers accompany them. All the teachers have the same number of students in their groups. How many students are in each group?

A	**B**	**C**	**D**	**E**
17	25	18	14	15

⑥ A ream of paper contains 500 sheets. For Louise's geography project she shares out one ream equally among 24 students. How many complete sheets does each student have?

A	**B**	**C**	**D**	**E**
20	15	18	21	28

⑦ Naomi bought a packet of 12 doughnuts for £3. What is the price of one doughnut?

A	**B**	**C**	**D**	**E**
36 p	30 p	24 p	21 p	25 p

⑧ Myra has asked John to sort out his garden shed. John collects a total of 578 loose nails. He purchases 17 small containers and fills each with the same number of nails. How many nails can each container hold?

A	**B**	**C**	**D**	**E**
36	41	33	34	43

⑨ In a maths challenge, Vijay has been asked to find the third dimension of a box with a volume of 120 cubic metres. He has been given two of the dimensions already. The area of one face is 24 metres squared. What is the correct length of the box?

A	B	C	D	E
8 m	2 m	4 m	3 m	5 m

⑩ A theatre is filled with drama students from 25 schools. Each coach transports the same number of student passengers from each school. There are 700 seats available for the students. How many students does each coach transport?

A	B	C	D	E
23	175	25	28	82

⑪ Mariam has a bag containing only square-based pyramids. In total, the bag contains 60 vertices. How many square-based pyramids does Miriam have?

A	B	C	D	E
15	12	10	18	13

⑫ At a summer camp, a total of 3 meals a day will be provided for each child. On average there will be 285 meals provided each day. How many children will attend, on average, each day?

A	B	C	D	E
75	78	85	95	97

⑬ An airport official calculated the total flight distance travelled by 42 planes. The total was 98 322 kilometres. What was the average distance travelled by each plane?

A	B	C	D	E
2341 km	3241 km	4321 km	1432 km	2431 km

⑭ Megan was working at a sheep farm over the summer. The farm had 1920 sheep. She had to work out $\frac{8}{30}$ of the flock that were to be sold to another farm. How many sheep was that?

A	B	C	D	E
64	84	640	512	240

⑮ Richard and Michael go on a fishing trip over 3 days. Richard catches a total of 33 fish and Michael a total of 51 fish. How many fish, on average, do they each catch per day?

A	B	C	D	E
28	42	14	24	41

Lesson 7: Multiplying and Dividing by 10, 100 and 1000

LEARN

Multiplying by 10, 100 and 1000

When multiplying by the **powers of 10** it is important to start at the decimal point. Look back to Lesson 1 to help you understand the value of different digits.

As you know, the position of the decimal point is 'fixed' (a bit like a drawing pin fixed to the wall) but there is a technique to help you. You may wish to consider this for the purpose of working out only.

When a number is multiplied, the value gets bigger.

If you multiply a number by **10**, the digits move to the left one place and grow in value ten times (or you can say the decimal point looks as if it moves or 'jumps' to the right one place, as there is one zero in 10).

If you multiply by **100**, the digits move to the left two places and grow in value a hundred times (or you can say the decimal point looks as if it moves or 'jumps' to the right two places, as there are two zeros in 100).

If you multiply by **1000**, the digits move to the left three places and grow in value a thousand times (or you can say the decimal point looks as if it moves or 'jumps' to the right three places, as there are three zeros in 1000).

This process of multiplying by the powers of 10 is illustrated below:

Example one: Simple multiplication with powers of 10, 100 and 1000

$4 \times 10 = 40$

$4 \times 100 = 400$

$4 \times 1000 = 4000$

$4.0. \quad \times 10 \quad = 4\,0. \quad$ or 4 0

$4.00. \quad \times 100 = 4\,0\,0. \quad$ or 4 0 0

$4.000. \times 1000 = 4\,0\,0\,0. \quad$ or 4 0 0 0

LEARN

Example two: Powers of 10 multiplication with a decimal point

2.4 × 10 = 24

2.4 × 100 = 240

2.4 × 1000 = 2400

2.4 × 10 = 24. or 24

2.40 × 100 = 240. or 240

2.400 × 1000 = 2400. or 2400

More examples:

31.64 × 10 = 316.4

0.71 × 100 = 71

0.82 × 1000 = 820

> The word multiplication starts with ⌢⌢↓ and you move or jump the decimal point to the right.

Dividing by 10, 100 and 1000

As division is the inverse of multiplication, the process uses the same principle but takes the 'opposite direction'. Therefore you move the numbers to the right, or 'jump' the decimal point to the left.

Example three: Simple division with powers of 10, 100 and 1000

4 ÷ 10 = 0.4

4 ÷ 100 = 0.04

4 ÷ 1000 = 0.004

4 ÷ 10 = 4. = 0.4

4 ÷ 100 = 04. = 0.04

4 ÷ 1000 = 004. = 0.004

More examples:

13.9 ÷ 10 = 1.39

13.9 ÷ 100 = 0.139

13.9 ÷ 1000 = 0.0139

DEVELOP

Try the following questions.

① 7.34 × 10 =

② 89.2 × 100 =

③ 0.03 × 1000 =

④ 8 ÷ 10 =

⑤ 65.7 ÷ 100 =

⑥ 5 ÷ 1000 =

⑦ 678 ÷ 100 =

⑧ 7.4 ÷ 1000 =

⑨ 2.1 × 1000 =

⑩ 0.8 × 1000 =

The decimal point is very powerful and its position determines the value of the number. You must therefore make it very clear. If the decimal point has no digit to the left, put a '0' (or 'bodyguard') to the left of the decimal, to help 'protect' the decimal point. For example, .34 now becomes 0.34

Lesson 8: Order of Operations (BIDMAS)

LEARN

If you are given a calculation with a mixture of operations, it is important to follow a rule. This rule ensures that **you do the operations in a certain order**. If the operations are not carried out in the correct order, then the answer will be wrong.

BIDMAS gives you the order in which operations should be carried out.
Remember BIDMAS stands for:

Brackets: if there are brackets, work out the value of the expression inside the brackets.

Indices: this includes powers, such as squared or cubed numbers, or square roots or cube roots.

Division: if there are no brackets or indices, do the division next.

Multiplication: has equal importance to division, so work from left to right to decide which to perform first.

Addition: if the expression only has addition and subtraction operations, then work from left to right.

Subtraction: has equal importance to addition, so work from left to right to decide which to perform first.

Example one:

$3 + (6 \div 3) - 1$

$= 3 + 2 - 1$

$= 5 - 1$

$= 4$

Example two:

$3 + 2 \times 5 - 1$

$= 3 + 10 - 1$

$= 13 - 1$

$= 12$

BIDMAS is a bit like baking a cake. You need to know what order to add the ingredients.

Example three:

$(8 + 2)^2 - 4 \times 3^2$

$= 10^2 - 4 \times 9$

$= 100 - 36$

$= 64$

DEVELOP

Use BIDMAS to answer the following questions.

① $3 \times 4^2 =$

② $30 \div (4 \div 2) + 3 =$

③ $20 \div 2^2 =$

④ $7 + 24 \div 6 =$

⑤ $(16 \div 8)^2 + 2 \times 3 =$

⑥ $3 \times (5^2 - 4^2) =$

⑦ $40 \div (12 - 4) =$

⑧ $(3 + 9) \div (3 + 1) =$

⑨ $2 + (2^3 \times 1) \times 4 =$

⑩ $2^2 \times (3 + 1^2)^3 =$

Other BIDMAS questions you could get are:

Make the expressions correct by replacing the * with + − × or ÷ and using brackets if required.

Example 1: $3 * 7 * 2 = 20$ becomes $(3 + 7) \times 2$

Example 2: $5 * 8 * 2 * 4 * 3 = 6$ becomes $5 + (8 \times 2) \div 4 - 3$

Try:

a) $4 * 2 * 8 = 10$

b) $5 * 4 * 6 * 8 = 21$

c) $2 * 6 * 3 * 4 = 10$

d) $1 * 3 * 8 * 6 * 2 = 3$

TIMED TEST 5

① Sarah's cake recipe requires 14 eggs. She is making a surprise cake for her mum's 50th birthday and needs to cater for a lot of guests. Sarah calculates she needs to make the cake 8 times bigger than the one in the recipe. If each egg costs 21 p, how much will she need to spend in total on the eggs?

A	B	C	D	E
£20.94	£2.94	£23.52	£1.68	£16.84

② Gareth takes 15 seconds to swim one length of the pool. If he swims for 5 minutes, how many lengths did he swim?

A	B	C	D	E
20	22	18	75	70

③ Anne was buying presents for her friends. She spent £24 on her best friend and half the amount on eight of her other friends. What is the maximum amount of £20 notes she could have used?

A	B	C	D	E
24	8	120	12	6

④ Molly, the dog, had a birthday party. Eleven other dogs attended her party. If there were five claws per paw, how many claws were there altogether at the party?

A	B	C	D	E
160	240	20	60	120

⑤ 'The Planets' is a piece of music composed by Gustav Holst. It is divided into seven sections, each named after a planet. The section called 'Mars' is 6 minutes and 7 seconds in length and the section called 'Venus' is 8 minutes and 23 seconds in length. What is the difference in length, in seconds, between the two sections?

A	B	C	D	E
306 s	503 s	367 s	136 s	186 s

⑥ A small bottle of oil contains 300 ml, a medium bottle contains 750 ml and a large bottle contains 1.5 litres. How many litres of oil do the three bottles contain altogether?

A	B	C	D	E
25 L	3.75 L	255 L	15.75 L	2.55 L

⑦ Oliver earns a total of £8.50 an hour for doing babysitting for his two sisters. He babysits for three hours a night for two evenings every week, for two years. On his final night he is given a £50 tip for all his fantastic work. How much does he earn altogether?

A	B	C	D	E
£5354	£5304	£1326	£6231	£75.50

⑧ Trevor is preparing his vegetable garden and plants cabbage out neatly in six rows. In each row there are 26 cabbages. He also plants lettuce in eight rows, with 18 in each row. He decides to dig two more rows and plants 32 cauliflowers in total. How many vegetables altogether has he planted?

A	B	C	D	E
364	330	332	188	176

⑨ Myra uses eight pineapples to make 600 ml of pineapple juice. How many pineapples would Myra need to use to make enough juice to fill eight 750 ml bottles?

A	B	C	D	E
80	24	93	10	40

⑩ There are 60 cows in a herd. Alice has been asked to milk the cows for three days in the school holidays. The total amount of milk produced by the herd in one day is 2280 litres. Over the three days how many litres of milk did each cow produce?

A	B	C	D	E
141 L	180 L	760 L	38 L	114 L

⑪ Hannah was raising money to go on a three-week school trip to South Africa. She decided to sell a range of toys. She had bought 28 of the toys for £1.25 each and all sold for £1.75 each. What was the total profit made from those particular toys?

A	B	C	D	E
£49	£14	£84	£78	£35

⑫ Last Wednesday $\frac{3}{8}$ of the pupils at Hafsah's school were absent. There are 560 children altogether at the school. How many pupils attended school that day?

A	B	C	D	E
70	140	350	210	280

⑬ Four supermarkets each order 36 crates of jam. Each crate holds 180 jars. How many jars altogether have the supermarkets ordered?

A	B	C	D	E
6480	25 920	12 960	720	24 860

⑭ Nishaan has 284 football cards. He puts them all in a scrapbook that contains 24 pages. Each page holds 12 cards. He fills all the pages except the last page. How many cards does Nishaan stick into the last page?

A	B	C	D	E
8	12	10	11	7

⑮ Ben has started his driving lessons. Each lesson costs £26. He has been given £85 for Christmas towards the lessons and £117 for his birthday towards the lessons. He aims to do a maximum of 12 lessons. How much more money has Ben got to save to afford the lessons?

A	B	C	D	E
£312	£202	£140	£110	£250

SECTION 2:

EQUIVALENT NUMBERS

Often when you first learn the basic fractions it can be easier to visualise them in a **fraction wall**. The image below can help you understand equivalent values. For example, how many eighths are in one quarter? The wall clearly shows $\frac{2}{8}$ is the same as $\frac{1}{4}$.

I whole											
$\frac{1}{2}$						$\frac{1}{2}$					
$\frac{1}{3}$				$\frac{1}{3}$				$\frac{1}{3}$			
$\frac{1}{4}$			$\frac{1}{4}$			$\frac{1}{4}$			$\frac{1}{4}$		
$\frac{1}{5}$		$\frac{1}{5}$		$\frac{1}{5}$			$\frac{1}{5}$		$\frac{1}{5}$		
$\frac{1}{6}$		$\frac{1}{6}$		$\frac{1}{6}$		$\frac{1}{6}$		$\frac{1}{6}$		$\frac{1}{6}$	
$\frac{1}{8}$	$\frac{1}{8}$		$\frac{1}{8}$	$\frac{1}{8}$		$\frac{1}{8}$	$\frac{1}{8}$		$\frac{1}{8}$	$\frac{1}{8}$	
$\frac{1}{10}$	$\frac{1}{10}$	$\frac{1}{10}$	$\frac{1}{10}$	$\frac{1}{10}$	$\frac{1}{10}$	$\frac{1}{10}$	$\frac{1}{10}$	$\frac{1}{10}$	$\frac{1}{10}$		
$\frac{1}{12}$	$\frac{1}{12}$	$\frac{1}{12}$	$\frac{1}{12}$	$\frac{1}{12}$	$\frac{1}{12}$	$\frac{1}{12}$	$\frac{1}{12}$	$\frac{1}{12}$	$\frac{1}{12}$	$\frac{1}{12}$	$\frac{1}{12}$

In this lesson you will be focusing on finding **fractions** of quantities and applying your knowledge of fractions to word problems. Firstly, you need to learn the correct terminology when solving fraction questions. The bottom number is called the 'denominator' and indicates how many parts you have altogether. The top number is referred to as the 'numerator' and it indicates how many parts of the whole you have.

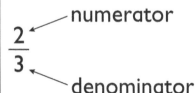

To find a fraction of a quantity, you need to divide the amount by the denominator and multiply by the numerator. You must always simplify the fraction to its lowest term.

Example:

In a school car park there were 56 cars. $\frac{3}{8}$ of them were red in colour. How many red cars were in the school car park?

$56 \div 8 = 7$ $7 \times 3 = 21$ 21 cars were red

DEVELOP

Find the fractions of the following quantities.

① $\frac{6}{7}$ of 42 =

② $\frac{4}{9}$ of 81 =

③ $\frac{8}{11}$ of 121 =

④ $\frac{5}{12}$ of 144 =

⑤ $\frac{7}{13}$ of 78 =

⑥ $\frac{9}{17}$ of 51 =

⑦ $\frac{12}{24}$ of 240 =

⑧ $\frac{4}{6}$ of 1200 =

⑨ $\frac{19}{25}$ of 3000 =

⑩ $\frac{27}{50}$ of 4000 =

Remember to divide the quantity by the denominator (bottom number) and multiply by the numerator (top number).

TIMED TEST 6

① A golfer hit 100 balls at the golf range. He hit $\frac{5}{25}$ of the balls over 250 yards. How many balls did he not hit that far?

A	B	C	D	E
60	40	20	80	30

② If $\frac{6}{7}$ of Lily's pocket money is £4.20, how much does she have in total?

A	B	C	D	E
£4.80	£4.50	£5.00	£4.40	£4.90

③ Jack's house is 600 m from his school. He walks to and from school every day. What fraction of 3 km does he walk in one day?

A	B	C	D	E
$\frac{2}{5}$	$\frac{3}{5}$	$\frac{1}{5}$	$\frac{3}{6}$	$\frac{4}{5}$

④ A baby slept for 8 hours every night. If the total number of sleeping hours was 56 in a week, what fraction of hours did the baby sleep on Tuesday and Wednesday?

A	B	C	D	E
$\frac{4}{7}$	$\frac{3}{7}$	$\frac{3}{8}$	$\frac{2}{7}$	$\frac{5}{8}$

⑤ An athlete drank 5 litres of water during an event. Each bottle holds 250 ml. In its simplest form, what fraction of the total drunk is four bottles?

A	B	C	D	E
$\frac{6}{20}$	$\frac{1}{10}$	$\frac{5}{20}$	$\frac{1}{5}$	$\frac{2}{10}$

⑥ On Bracken Farm there are 51 sheep, 20 cows, 19 ducks and 5 horses. What fraction of the animals are ducks?

A	B	C	D	E
$\frac{1}{4}$	$\frac{1}{5}$	$\frac{1}{6}$	$\frac{2}{5}$	$\frac{4}{6}$

⑦ Nigel spends 3 hours on the train every week day. What fraction of the day does Nigel spend on the train?

A	B	C	D	E
$\frac{1}{4}$	$\frac{1}{8}$	$\frac{4}{24}$	$\frac{3}{12}$	$\frac{6}{6}$

⑧ How many thirds are there in $6\frac{2}{3}$?

A	B	C	D	E
18	20	30	22	24

⑨ Brian has $\frac{3}{4}$ kg of liquorice allsorts. If he gives $\frac{1}{8}$ kg to Alex, what fraction will he have left?

A	B	C	D	E
$\frac{5}{8}$	$\frac{4}{8}$	$\frac{1}{8}$	$\frac{2}{8}$	$\frac{3}{8}$

⑩ Jason spends $\frac{1}{3}$ of his pocket money on clothes and $\frac{2}{5}$ on stationery for school. If he had £45 to spend, how much money does Jason have left?

A	B	C	D	E
£24	£18	£12	£15	£40

⑪ A car journey is 120 miles. Anita has driven $\frac{3}{5}$ of the journey before she needs to get fuel. How many miles are left in the journey?

A	B	C	D	E
40 miles	24 miles	72 miles	12 miles	48 miles

⑫ A farmer owns 480 hectares of land. He plants swedes on $\frac{4}{16}$ of his land. On the rest of the farm he grows wheat. How many hectares does he use for wheat?

A	B	C	D	E
320h	340h	360h	120h	300h

⑬ An engineer tests 900 components on a new aircraft. On day 1 she checks $\frac{3}{12}$ of the parts and on the following day $\frac{2}{12}$. How many parts does the engineer have left to test?

A	B	C	D	E
525	400	375	300	3000

⑭ Louise places an advert in a local magazine. The cost of the advert is £20 for each $\frac{1}{8}$ of a page. An advert uses $\frac{6}{16}$ of a page. How much does the advert cost?

A	B	C	D	E
£50	£60	£80	£30	£70

⑮ In a recent survey, 500 people were asked how they would vote in the next election. These were the results:

220 Conservative

200 Labour

80 Other

What fraction of the total would vote 'other'?

A	B	C	D	E
$\frac{1}{5}$	$\frac{1}{4}$	$\frac{4}{25}$	$\frac{1}{6}$	$\frac{6}{25}$

Lesson 10: Decimals

LEARN

Decimals are numbers that are between two whole numbers. For example, 4.2 is between the numbers 4 and 5. It is more than 4 but less than 5. You can use the knowledge gained in Lesson 1 to help you in this section.

Let's look at a decimal number:

6.75

- The number to the left of the decimal point is a whole number.

- The numbers to the right of the decimal point are parts of a whole number.

When comparing decimal numbers, it is important to make sure the **decimal points** line up. Let's compare 5.671 and 5.617 to see which number is the largest. Take a look at the table below. Both the units and the tenths columns have the same digits, so you need to look at the hundredths column: 5.671 is larger as it has seven hundredths whereas 5.617 only has one hundredth. In this example there is no need to compare the thousandths column.

units (ones)	decimal point	tenths	hundredths	thousandths
5	.	6	7	1
5	.	6	1	7

It is important that you can add, subtract, multiply and divide decimal numbers in 11+ maths. When adding or subtracting, you can use the same methods that you learnt in the earlier lessons.

Remember to always keep the decimal point in the same column when adding and subtracting decimal numbers.

DEVELOP

Have a go at these decimal questions.

① Calculate 3.24 + 2.67

② Add together 6.95 and 7.67

③ What is the difference between 8.94 and 7.5?

④ By how much is 9.8 greater than 0.7?

⑤ Subtract 19.43 and 12.98 from 40

⑥ What is 18 ÷ 0.9?

⑦ Work out 0.7 × 1.5

⑧ Total 123.56, 10.23 and 2.09

⑨ What is the product of 4.5 and 4.5?

⑩ Calculate 8.65 + 5.43

Make sure you understand the value of each digit, e.g. tenth, hundredth, thousandth.

TIMED TEST 7

15:00
15 minutes

① What is the product of 1.5 × 1.5?

A	**B**	**C**	**D**	**E**
2.35	2.45	3	2.55	2.25

② Find the difference between 0.2 and 0.02

A	**B**	**C**	**D**	**E**
0.17	0.16	0.18	0.01	0.04

③ What must be added to 38.2 to equal 50?

A	**B**	**C**	**D**	**E**
11.7	11.8	11.6	12	11.5

④ Which decimal number is the median in this list?

3.03   3.33   3.3   3.42   3.333

A	**B**	**C**	**D**	**E**
3.03	3.33	3.3	3.42	3.333

⑤ Calculate 93.41 + 5.6

A	**B**	**C**	**D**	**E**
99.01	99.02	99.03	98.02	98.03

⑥ What is 6 ÷ 1.2?

A	**B**	**C**	**D**	**E**
4	3	2	5	6

⑦ What is the total of £3.21 + £0.78 + £6.01?

A	**B**	**C**	**D**	**E**
£10	£11	£9	£12	£8

⑧ What is the sum of the following measurements?

1.45 m   0.35 m   152 cm

A	**B**	**C**	**D**	**E**
3.33 m	3.32 m	15.45 m	3.52 m	3.34 m

⑨ Three athletes competed in a long jump competition. They jumped 7.70 m, 7.99 m and 8.01 m. What was the mean?

A	**B**	**C**	**D**	**E**
8.0 m	8.1 m	8.2 m	7.8 m	7.9 m

⑩ Start at 12.6 and count back 15 tenths. What number do you finish on?

A	**B**	**C**	**D**	**E**
11.3	11.1	2.4	11.2	12.1

⑪ Calculate 7 ÷ 0.5

A	**B**	**C**	**D**	**E**
4	14	15	16	17

⑫ A bottle holds 330 ml of tomato juice. How many bottles can be made from 1.7 litres?

A	**B**	**C**	**D**	**E**
6	4	5	7	8

⑬ Bella saved some of her pocket money for six weeks.
She saved: 88p   £8   80p   £8.08   888p   £0.80
How much did she save altogether?

A	**B**	**C**	**D**	**E**
£27.43	£27.44	£28.44	£27.40	£28.09

⑭ Jake had 1.2 litres of orange juice and James had 800 ml of apple juice. John drank 100 cl of grapefruit juice. How much juice was consumed altogether?

A	**B**	**C**	**D**	**E**
3 L	3.02 L	3.04 L	3.05 L	3.1 L

⑮ Calculate 1.1 × 1.1 × 1.1

A	**B**	**C**	**D**	**E**
13.33	1.321	1.334	1.331	133.1

LEARN

In this lesson you will be solving percentage problems. It is important to understand that 'per cent' means '**out of 100**'. If there were a possible 100 marks on a test and you scored 85, your percentage score would be 85%.

So $85\% = \frac{85}{100}$

Having a secure understanding of your factors of 100 will help you solve many percentage questions. Below are listed the factors of 100:

1, 2, 4, 5, 10, 20, 25, 50, 100

Thinking of the factors in pairs, 1×100, 2×50, 4×25, 5×20 and 10×10, will help you decipher many different percentage questions.

Example

What is 13 out of 20 as a percentage?

Let's imagine you have scored 13 out of 20 in a spelling test at school and we need to record the answer as a percentage. The number 20 has a factor pair of 5 and this can be useful to convert this raw score into a percentage. See the method below:

$$\frac{13}{20} \times 5 = \frac{65}{100} = 65\%$$

It is important to realise that to find 1% of a number you divide by 100 and to find 10% of a number you divide by 10. In the 'Develop' section, see if you can use these key facts to help you.

DEVELOP

Find the following percentages of these amounts.

①   10% of 80 =

②   15% of 60 =

③   20% of 120 =

④   35% of 200 =

⑤   50% of 1500 =

⑥   70% of 3000 =

⑦   5% of 300 =

⑧   6% of 900 =

⑨   23% of 150 =

⑩   46% of 800 =

A useful tip when trying to find 5% of a number is to find 10% first and then halve the answer.

TIMED TEST 8

15:00
15 minutes

① There are 200 children at Highpoint School. 2% of the students were absent on one day. How many children were present?

A	**B**	**C**	**D**	**E**
4	196	190	8	2

② There were 600 children's books in the local library. 180 of them were non-fiction, the rest were fiction. What percentage were fiction books?

A	**B**	**C**	**D**	**E**
60%	50%	70%	65%	30%

③ A mahogany table costs £120, but you need to add 20% VAT. What is its actual price?

A	**B**	**C**	**D**	**E**
£96	£140	£132	£144	£100

④ In a Science test out of 80, Catherine scored 60. What percentage is this?

A	**B**	**C**	**D**	**E**
25%	75%	60%	80%	65%

⑤ In a sale, a jacket usually costing £160 is reduced by 25%. What is the new cost of the coat?

A	**B**	**C**	**D**	**E**
£120	£140	£135	£125	£180

⑥ The cost of a garden shed is £300 in September but it will increase by 15% in October. How much will the garden shed cost in October?

A	**B**	**C**	**D**	**E**
£255	£315	£285	£310	£345

⑦ Henry bought a car for £4200 but, after making some repairs, he sold it for 21% more than he purchased it for. What was the new sale price?

A	**B**	**C**	**D**	**E**
£4620	£5082	£4242	£4221	£5042

⑧ A hospital contains 320 beds. If 25% are empty, how many are being used?

A	**B**	**C**	**D**	**E**
400	260	240	460	230

⑨ A savings account pays interest of 4%. How much will be in the account after the interest is added to £1800?

A	B	C	D	E
£1818	£1872	£1836	£1804	£1796

⑩ A laptop computer costs £1100. It is reduced by 5% in a sale. What is the sale price of the computer?

A	B	C	D	E
£1035	£1045	£1055	£1020	£1030

⑪ Barrie decides to invest £3500 in a pension scheme and earn 8% interest. How much interest does he receive?

A	B	C	D	E
£250	£270	£260	£240	£280

⑫ Susanna's hourly wage rises from £7.20 to £7.92. What percentage increase is this?

A	B	C	D	E
8%	5%	10%	6%	7%

⑬ A cheese-burger, chips and a drink cost £4.50, but from tomorrow the price will increase by 10%. What will be the new cost of the meal?

A	B	C	D	E
£4.95	£4.05	£4.55	£4.00	£5.05

⑭ A colony of 300 Emperor penguins was depleted by 7% due to severe weather. How many Emperor penguins were left in the group?

A	B	C	D	E
270	279	293	260	278

⑮ The Smith family purchased a house for £250000 five years ago. They sell the property for £450000. What was the percentage increase?

A	B	C	D	E
50%	60%	80%	90%	40%

**THIS PAGE HAS DELIBERATELY
BEEN LEFT BLANK**

SECTION 3:

ALGEBRA

LEARN

The **nth term** is a rule, or expression, to describe the number pattern of a sequence. It can be used to find any number (or term) in a number sequence.

You may be given the first five terms of a sequence and then be asked to find the 20th term or 50th term, for example.

The *n*th term can also be used to identify whether a number is in the sequence.

Example one

| *n* | = | the number in the sequence |

n	=	1	2	3	4	$\longrightarrow$
term	=	2	4	6	8	

At this level in maths, you will be given an *n*th term expression (or rule). With the above example, the *n*th term is $2n$ because:

n	=	$1_{\times 2}$	$2_{\times 2}$	$3_{\times 2}$	$4_{\times 2}$	$20_{\times 2}$	$100_{\times 2}$
term	=	2	4	6	8	40	200

You could be asked to work out any term in the sequence using the rule $2n$.

Example two

n	=	$1n^2$	$2n^2$	$3n^2$	$4n^2$	$30n^2$	$50n^2$
term	=	1	4	9	16	900	2500

The *n*th term expression (or rule) here is n^2.

You could be asked to find the 30th term using the rule.

Tip: If you are asked to recognise what expression describes the sequence, it is a good idea to number (*n*) each term of the sequence 1, 2, 3, etc.

DEVELOP

For questions 1, 2 and 3, look at the sequence and select the expression which could be used to find the *n*th term.

① 2,   5,   8,   11,   14

   A $3n - 4$ **C** $n + 1$

   B n^2 **D** $3n - 1$

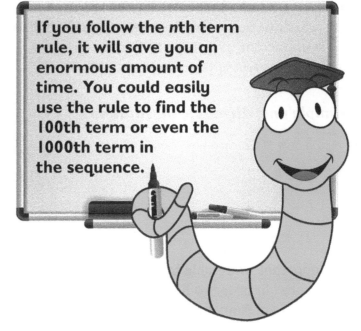

If you follow the *n*th term rule, it will save you an enormous amount of time. You could easily use the rule to find the 100th term or even the 1000th term in the sequence.

② 9,   16,   25,   36,   49

   A $n \div 2$ **C** $(n + 2)^2$

   B $4n$ **D** $(n^2 + 2)$

③ −2,   1,   6,   13,   22

   A $n - 3$ **C** $(2n) - 1$

   B $(n + 1)^2$ **D** $n^2 - 3$

④ What is the 4th term when using the expression $n \div 2 + 1$?

⑤ Write the 10th term for the expression $4n - 2$

⑥ What is the 5th term of the sequence with the *n*th term rule $n^2 - 5$?

⑦ Write the 100th term for the expression $2(n - 1)$

⑧ Write the 15th term for the expression $4n - 3$

⑨ What position is 100 in the sequence given by the rule n^2?

⑩ With the expression $6n - 4$, is it correct to say the 3rd term is 14? Yes or no.

Lesson 13: Introduction to Algebra

LEARN

Algebra is where shapes or letters are used instead of numbers: this is called **algebraic substitution**. Below are some examples of substitutions with shapes or letters as numbers. This is important as it helps to find the unknown. You can use algebra in real-life problems and use equations to try to solve them.

Example one: Algebraic substitution

① $3 \triangle 4 = 12$ $\triangle = \times$

② $8 \, ☆ \, 4 = 2$ $☆ = \div$

③ $6 \times t = 24$ $t = 4$

④ $21 \div a = 7$ $a = 3$

It is important to be able to simplify algebra, especially when the equations become more complicated in order to help work out the answer. Let's look at some examples – it's all about collecting 'like' (same) terms.

Example two: Simplifying expressions

① $T + T + T = 3T$

② $H + H + W + W = 2H + 2W$

③ $3 \times n = 3n$

④ $8 \div J = \dfrac{8}{J}$

⑤ $X \times Y \times Z = XYZ$

⑥ $3 \times R + 2 = 3R + 2$

In algebra you don't use multiplication signs as it looks like a letter. You just write the number before the letter.

DEVELOP

Can you work out what numbers the letters represent below?

① $M \times 8 = 16$ What is M?

② $28 \div t = 4$ What is t?

③ $5 + w = 14$ What is w?

④ $46 - y = 25$ What is y?

⑤ $H \div 5 = 9$ What is H?

Algebraic substitution questions could also start with known values of letters. For example, if $P = 8$ and $Q = 9$, what is $P + Q$? The answer is 17.

With the values of A, B, C given below, try the following questions.

$A = 5$ $B = 6$ $C = 10$

⑥ $A + B =$

⑦ $3B =$

⑧ $AB \div 3 =$

⑨ $A + 2B + C =$

⑩ $BC - A =$

Below are some questions for you to try to simplify.

⑪ $d + d =$

⑫ $c + c + c =$

⑬ $14k \div 7 =$

⑭ $16d \div d =$

⑮ $12y \div 4y =$

LEARN

Algebraic equations are also known as 'balanced' equations as the value on the left side of the equals sign is the same as on the right.

A bit like balancing the equation on a set of weighing scales.

Example one: 4x = 20

The aim is to solve the equation and find the value of the 'unknown' or letter, which in this example is x. The letter needs to be on one side of the equals sign and the numbers on the other.

$4x = 20$

You need to make the 4 on the left of the equals sign 'magically disappear' and 'reappear' on the right side of the sign. This is done by cancelling out the multiplication. You can cancel out the multiplication of 4 by the inverse operation, division.

$x = 20 \div 4$

$x = 5$

Check whether the answer is correct, $4 \times 5 = 20$

The inverse of multiplication is division. The inverse of addition is subtraction.

LEARN

Example two: 2p + 3 = 13

What is the value of *p*? The aim is to get rid of the 'floater' number (+ 3) first. You need to make it magically disappear by cancelling it out. The inverse of + 3 is − 3.

$2p + 3 = 13$

$2p = 13 − 3$

$2p = 10$

Then we need to make the '2' on the left vanish and reappear on the right of the equals sign. $2p$ means *p* is multiplied by 2, therefore the inverse would be to divide by 2.

$2p = 10$

$p = 10 ÷ 2$

$p = 5$

Then check whether *p* is 5 by substituting *p* with 5. This is $2 × 5 + 3 = 13$

Example three: C ÷ 4 − 2 = 1

Get rid of the 'floater' first.

$C ÷ 4 − 2 = 1$

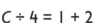 $+ 2 \quad + 2$ ⬅ Balance out the 'floater' by adding 2 to each side

$C ÷ 4 = 1 + 2$

$C ÷ 4 = 3$

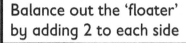 $× 4 \quad × 4$ ⬅ Balance further by multiplying each side by 4

$C = 3 × 4$

$C = 12$

Check your answer by substituting C with 12:

$12 ÷ 4 − 2 = 1$

$C = 12$

LEARN

Example four: Linear equations

In the 11+ exam, you may need to solve a linear equation. This is an equation connecting two variables that give a straight line when plotted on a graph. There are often unknowns on both sides of the equals sign.

Get the letters to one side (on the left) and the numbers on the other (to the right).

$6m - 17 = m + 3$

$6m - m - 17 = 3$

$5m = 3 + 17$

$5m = 20$

$m = 20 \div 5$

$m = 4$

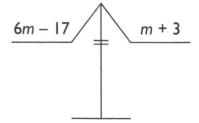

Check your answer using the substitution process:

$(6 \times 4) - 17 = 4 + 3$

$7 = 7$

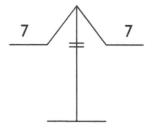

Example five: Applying algebraic knowledge to word problems

Audrey had six house points. From her history project she has just been given more house points (H). She now has 10 house points. How many house points (H) was Audrey awarded for history?

The 'unknown' is the number of house points (H) and you can translate the question into a maths algebraic equation:

$6 + H = 10$

$H = 10 - 6$

$H = 4$

Answer: Audrey was awarded 4 house points for history.

DEVELOP

Have a go at solving the following algebraic equations.

① $2y + 5 = 17$ $y =$

② $5R - 9 = 31$ $R =$

③ $14n - 20 = 22$ $n =$

④ $41 = 7M + 6$ $M =$

⑤ $9 + 16W = 73$ $W =$

⑥ $\dfrac{R}{8} + 6 = 10$ $R =$

⑦ $\dfrac{J}{7} - 5 = 3$ $J =$

⑧ $\dfrac{T}{24} + 28 = 32$ $T =$

⑨ $7y - 11 = y + 1$ $y =$

⑩ $17x - 6 = 9x + 2$ $x =$

TIMED TEST 9

① With the expression $n^3 + 1$, what is the 5th term?

A	B	C	D	E
124	116	120	126	130

② What is the 15th term for the expression $4n - 3$?

A	B	C	D	E
57	63	37	42	48

③ If $A = 3$, $B = 8$ and $C = 10$, what is the answer for $(B + C)A$?

A	B	C	D	E
40	60	38	45	54

④ What is the answer after simplifying $6 \times e - 2 \times e$?

A	B	C	D	E
8e	7e	4e	4e + 2	6e – 2

⑤ Simplify $g + g + 2 \times h + g$

A	B	C	D	E
2g + 2h + g	3g 2h	3g × 2h	3g + 2h	2g × 2h + g

⑥ What does A stand for in the following equation?
$A \div 10 - 5 = 5$

A	B	C	D	E
5	50	100	75	10

⑦ Sarah plays a game of thinking of a number. She then halves it and takes 16 from it. She is left with 34. What number was she thinking of?

A	B	C	D	E
150	100	50	68	32

⑧ When Kieran got his pocket money, he spent £2.30 on sweets and had £4.20 left. How much pocket money did he get?

A	B	C	D	E
£4.60	£4.30	£4.20	£6.50	£6.20

(9) Stacey is preparing for an Easter gathering. She makes 12 hot cross buns and 16 chocolate nests. She eats 2 chocolate nests as she is feeling hungry. She makes gingerbread bunny biscuits and an Easter cake. If she puts 56 different treats on the table, how many bunny biscuits did she make?

A	B	C	D	E
29	56	41	39	51

(10) Heather wanted to knit a nativity scene for Christmas. She bought 22 balls of wool in total: 6 were beige, 4 green, 2 brown, 5 purple, 2 yellow and the rest were red. How many balls of wool were red?

A	B	C	D	E
29	19	13	22	3

(11) Olly bought 4 football tickets. They each cost £F. He had to pay a booking fee of £7 and four train tickets that each cost £15. His total expense was £195. How much was one football ticket?

A	B	C	D	E
£195	£188	£32	£128	£38

(12) Ann had a bag of grapes. She ate 6, gave 8 to each of her two siblings, and gave the remaining 22 to her mum for her pavlova pudding. How many grapes did Ann start with?

A	B	C	D	E
24	44	30	22	54

(13) Ben started with 15 tennis balls this season. He lost a few and was left with six. He gives half of his remaining balls to his cousin, and keeps three. How many balls did he lose?

A	B	C	D	E
9	6	12	10	8

(14) Bill is $2\frac{1}{2}$ times older than his son, Louie. Bill is 50. How old is Louie?

A	B	C	D	E
27	18	20	25	32

(15) If you treble Nisha's age and add 11, you have her mother's age of 50. How old is Nisha?

A	B	C	D	E
11	15	14	53	13

THIS PAGE HAS DELIBERATELY BEEN LEFT BLANK

SECTION 4:

STATISTICS

LEARN

In this section you will be learning about statistics; that is different ways of analysing data in large quantities. There are four lessons and the first one is on Ratio and Proportion.

Ratios

Ratios demonstrate the **relationship between two numbers** and how they compare to one another. Examples of ratios can be seen in many everyday situations, for instance when mixing up squash. If it states on the bottle 1 part squash to 4 parts water, it is important to add the correct quantities.

We often represent ratios as two numbers with a colon in between, for example 3 : 4.

For example: The diagram below has a ratio of 3 : 4 and means 3 to every 4. For every 3 red squares there are 4 blue triangles.

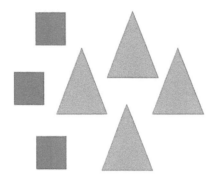

When something is shared in a ratio, it helps to find out how many equal parts there are in total. In the above ratio, this would mean adding 3 + 4 together to equal 7. In the example about squash above, there are 5 parts in total (1 + 4).

1 FREE child ticket for every 2 adult tickets bought

If you see the above sign outside a cinema, it can be represented as 1 : 2.

To find an equivalent ratio, you must multiply or divide both sides by the same number. Therefore, using the cinema ticket scenario again, if you had 4 adults going to watch the film you are entitled to 2 free child tickets.

2 : 4 = 2 free child tickets for every 4 adult tickets.

4 : 8 = 4 free child tickets for every 8 adult tickets.

LEARN

Sometimes ratios can be shown with more than two numbers. For example, if we had a concrete mix containing cement, sand and stones, a typical mix might be in a ratio of 1 : 2 : 6. For every set quantity of cement, you require double the amount of sand and six times the amount of stones.

Proportion

A proportion of something is a way of describing **a part of a whole**. You can find the word 'proportion' in everyday situations. For example, if you bake a cake, quantities in the recipe are increased in proportion if a bigger cake is needed.

$$\frac{1}{3} = \frac{2}{6}$$
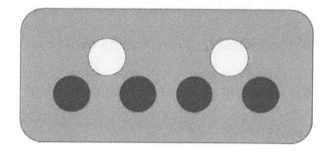

Two quantities are in direct proportion when they increase or decrease in the same ratio. For example, if there are 4 boys to every 3 girls in a class, the proportion of 8 boys to every 6 girls would be the same. The two ratios are the same, 4 : 3 and 8 : 6, but the first is written in the simplest form.

An example of a proportion-style question:

If 12 pencils cost 60 p, how much would 15 pencils cost?

First, work out the cost of one pencil, which is 60 ÷ 12 = 5 p. Then, to find the cost of 15 pencils, multiply 15 by 5. This equals 75 p.

DEVELOP

Write these statements as ratios.

①   3 oranges were eaten to every 5 pears

②   On a necklace there were 6 emeralds to every 4 rubies

③   In a suitcase there were 7 socks to every 2 t-shirts packed

④   I cm on a diagram represents 250 cm in real life

⑤   10 footballs were kicked at the goal to every 3 saved

Write the following ratios in their simplest form.

⑥   48 : 16

⑦   72 : 18

⑧   56 : 49

⑨   108 : 84

⑩   250 : 1000

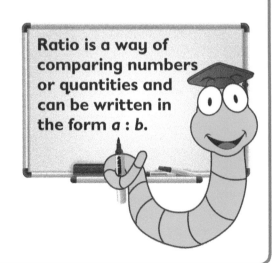

Ratio is a way of comparing numbers or quantities and can be written in the form *a* : *b*.

TIMED TEST 10

Circle the letter above the correct answer with a pencil.

① £2.40 is shared between Jessica, Daisy and Olivia in the ratio 3 : 2 : 1. How much does Daisy receive?

A	B	C	D	E
40p	80p	£1.20	£1.60	20p

② A bag of sweets is shared between Arzaan, Rory and Finley in the ratio of 5 : 3 : 1. There are 54 sweets. How many does Arzaan receive?

A	B	C	D	E
60	6	18	30	24

③ Arran and Kushi win £1000 between them. They agree to divide the money in the ratio 2 : 3. How much does Kushi receive?

A	B	C	D	E
£200	£400	£600	£800	£750

④ A necklace is made with silver and gold beads in the ratio of 7 : 3. There are 90 beads in the necklace. How many are silver?

A	B	C	D	E
27	45	64	54	63

⑤ On a map, the scale is 1 cm = 100 km. What would be the distance in metres for a 5 cm length on the map?

A	B	C	D	E
500 000 m	50 000 m	5000 m	500 m	50 m

⑥ An orange is divided in the ratio 4 : 2 : 1. If there are 14 segments in total, how many pieces represent the largest share?

A	B	C	D	E
2	6	7	8	4

⑦ A pack of 52 playing cards are dealt out in piles in the ratio 7 : 4 : 2. How many cards are in the smallest pile?

A	B	C	D	E
9	8	16	28	13

⑧ At a party, 108 biscuits were shared in the ratio 2 : 3 : 1. How many biscuits did the group who had 2 parts receive?

A	B	C	D	E
28	54	36	18	90

⑨ In a cricket test series, the runs scored by Freddie, Jimmy and Joe were shared in a ratio of 3 : 2 : 2. If 560 runs were scored, how many runs did Freddie score?

A	B	C	D	E
160	320	250	400	240

⑩ In a school car park the colours of the vehicles were green, red, silver, black and blue. The car park had 55 cars in the ratio 1 : 4 : 2 : 1 : 3. How many red cars were in the car park?

A	B	C	D	E
15	20	25	5	48

⑪ A model train is made using a plan with a scale of 1 : 30. This means every 1 cm represents 30 cm. How long in metres would a model train be if it measured 5 cm on the plan?

A	B	C	D	E
150 cm	1.3 m	1.5 m	30 m	50 m

⑫ Grace divided 144 sweets between her grandchildren in the ratio of 1 : 2 : 3 : 4 : 1 : 1 according to their age. What was the greatest number of sweets received by one of her grandchildren?

A	B	C	D	E
48	24	60	12	72

⑬ A moorland map is drawn to a scale of 1 cm = 9 km. A distance of 7.5 cm on the map represents how many kilometres of the moor?

A	B	C	D	E
65.5 km	63.5 km	66.5 km	67.5 km	68.5 km

⑭ At a fairground, 240 litres of pineapple squash were made up in the ratio 3 : 5, 3 parts pineapple squash and 5 parts water. How much water was added?

A	B	C	D	E
90 L	150 L	120 L	180 L	130 L

⑮ Kajol has a bag of 70 sweets. She keeps 10 for herself and gives $\frac{1}{3}$ of the remaining sweets to her brother, Rajan. The other sweets are shared between Kajol's dad and mum in a ratio of 6 : 2. How many sweets does her dad receive?

A	B	C	D	E
40	20	60	30	50

LEARN

Probability is the **likelihood or chance** of something happening. In our everyday language we use probability terms like certain, unlikely or improbable. One common situation when we describe the chance of something happening is the weather.

'It is unlikely to rain today in the south-east'

You can use fractions, decimals or percentages to describe probability. This probability scale helps you to understand the relationship between these different areas of maths.

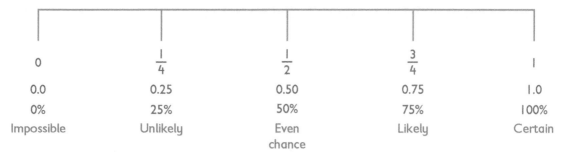

0	$\frac{1}{4}$	$\frac{1}{2}$	$\frac{3}{4}$	1
0.0	0.25	0.50	0.75	1.0
0%	25%	50%	75%	100%
Impossible	Unlikely	Even chance	Likely	Certain

When solving probability questions, you need to consider the number of possible outcomes. For example, if you roll a die you could get 1, 2, 3, 4, 5 or 6. These are referred to as outcomes. There is an equal chance of rolling any of these numbers (outcomes).

So, if you throw two dice, what is the probability of getting a 6 on both dice? When you roll two dice, there are now 36 different and unique ways the dice can fall. This figure is arrived at by multiplying the number of ways the first die can fall (six) by the number of ways the second die can come up (six). 6 × 6 = 36. Therefore, there is a 1 in 36 ($\frac{1}{36}$) chance of rolling two 6s on two dice.

The probability of an outcome = $\dfrac{\text{number of ways the outcome could happen}}{\text{total number of possible outcomes}}$

DEVELOP

Find the probability of the following events.

① The likelihood of rolling a prime number on a die.

② Choosing a red pencil from a pack of 2 blue, 3 green, 4 yellow and 3 red.

③ The chance of three coins all landing on tails.

④ Choosing a day of the week at random.

⑤ Out of the numbers 1 to 10, choosing a squared number.

Answer the following probability questions based on this spinner. Give answers as a fraction.

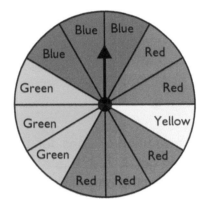

⑥ What is the likelihood of getting a red on the spinner?

⑦ What is the chance of getting a yellow on the spinner?

⑧ What is the chance of getting a blue or a green colour?

⑨ What is the likelihood of landing on any colour except blue?

⑩ What is the chance of getting any colour except yellow?

You can often use a probability scale. 1 is certain and 0 is impossible.

TIMED TEST 11

15:00
15 minutes

In a bag there are 5 white balls, 2 green balls and 1 red ball.

1. What is the probability of picking out a red or a white ball?

A	**B**	**C**	**D**	**E**
$\frac{1}{4}$	$\frac{1}{2}$	$\frac{5}{8}$	$\frac{3}{4}$	$\frac{7}{8}$

2. If one white ball is removed, what is the chance of picking out a white ball?

A	**B**	**C**	**D**	**E**
$\frac{2}{8}$	$\frac{3}{8}$	$\frac{4}{7}$	$\frac{1}{2}$	$\frac{2}{7}$

A pack of 52 cards contains suits of clubs, hearts, diamonds and spades. There are 4 Aces, 4 Kings, 4 Queens and 4 Jacks in each pack.

3. What is the probability of picking out an ace?

A	**B**	**C**	**D**	**E**
$\frac{1}{13}$	$\frac{1}{5}$	$\frac{2}{13}$	$\frac{1}{7}$	$\frac{4}{26}$

4. What is the likelihood of selecting a picture card (Jack, Queen or King)?

A	**B**	**C**	**D**	**E**
$\frac{16}{52}$	$\frac{20}{52}$	$\frac{32}{50}$	$\frac{12}{52}$	$\frac{36}{52}$

5. What is the probability that you will pick a King of Diamonds?

A	**B**	**C**	**D**	**E**
$\frac{4}{52}$	$\frac{13}{52}$	$\frac{1}{52}$	$\frac{6}{52}$	$\frac{3}{52}$

Katie's CD player is on the random choice option. There are 15 songs in total: 6 pop songs, 3 slow songs, 4 hip-hop songs and 2 house tunes.

6. What is the probability of the song being either a slow song or a house tune?

A	**B**	**C**	**D**	**E**
$\frac{5}{12}$	$\frac{1}{3}$	$\frac{6}{15}$	$\frac{1}{4}$	$\frac{8}{15}$

7. What is the likelihood of the song not being hip-hop?

A	**B**	**C**	**D**	**E**
$\frac{6}{15}$	$\frac{1}{2}$	$\frac{4}{15}$	$\frac{9}{15}$	$\frac{11}{15}$

In the school's pencil box there were 5 red pencils, 2 blue pencils, 8 yellow pencils, 15 black pencils and 6 green pencils. When the box was new, there were 50 pencils.

⑧ What is the probability of picking out a blue pencil at random?

A	B	C	D	E
$\frac{2}{50}$	$\frac{1}{25}$	$\frac{2}{34}$	$\frac{1}{18}$	$\frac{4}{36}$

⑨ What is the likelihood of choosing a red or blue pencil out of the box?

A	B	C	D	E
$\frac{7}{50}$	$\frac{7}{36}$	$\frac{1}{4}$	$\frac{1}{6}$	$\frac{5}{36}$

⑩ If 10 black pencils are lost from the box, what is the new probability of a green pencil being chosen at random in its simplest form?

A	B	C	D	E
$\frac{6}{26}$	$\frac{6}{50}$	$\frac{3}{25}$	$\frac{6}{40}$	$\frac{3}{13}$

⑪ A company makes calculators. The company knows that the probability that a calculator will be defective is $\frac{1}{20}$. If a box contains 1000 calculators, how many are likely to be defective?

A	B	C	D	E
50	750	20	40	100

⑫ A bag holds 1 yellow and 4 green balls. A ball is taken out from the bag and is not replaced. Another ball is then taken out at random. If the first ball taken out is yellow, what is the probability that the second ball taken out is green?

A	B	C	D
probable	unlikely	certain	likely

⑬ A box of chocolates contains milk and dark chocolates. The chance of getting a milk chocolate is $\frac{6}{36}$. What is the probability of getting a dark chocolate?

A	B	C	D	E
$\frac{4}{6}$	$\frac{28}{26}$	$\frac{31}{36}$	$\frac{5}{6}$	$\frac{11}{12}$

⑭ If three coins are thrown, what is the probability of exactly two coins landing heads up?

A	B	C	D	E
$\frac{3}{8}$	$\frac{1}{3}$	$\frac{1}{2}$	$\frac{2}{3}$	$\frac{1}{4}$

⑮ If four dice are thrown at once, what is the probability of throwing 4 ones?

A	B	C	D	E
$\frac{1}{4}$	$\frac{1}{1296}$	$\frac{1}{1210}$	$\frac{4}{1296}$	$\frac{1}{36}$

LEARN

Finding averages and a range are often tested in an 11+ exam. Let's check you know what each type of average and the range means. There are three different types of averages of a set of data: the **mean**, the **median** and the **mode**.

Mean: Add together the numbers in the set of data and divide the total by how many numbers are in the set.

Example one: Working out the mean

In a mental arithmetic test, a group of pupils got these marks:

21, 22, 19, 18, 20

The total is 100 and there are 5 pupils. Therefore, the mean number of marks is 100 ÷ 5 = 20

Median: The median is the middle number. To find this, you need to reorder the numbers in the set in order of size. Find the middle number. If there are two middle numbers, you have to add those two numbers together and divide by 2.

Example two: Working out the median

Below is the number of miles driven each day by an electrician:

18, 3, 24, 16, 17, 23, 9

The data set reordered is:

3, 9, 16, 17, 18, 23, 24

17 is the median number of miles.

Mode: To find this type of average, you find the number that appears most frequently in the set of data.

Example three: Working out the mode

A set of temperatures recorded in degrees Celsius during one week in Maidenhead were:

16, 15, 14, 13, 15, 14, 14

14 degrees Celsius is the modal temperature as it appears most often.

Range: To find the range of a set of data, simply find the difference between the smallest value and the largest value.

Example four: Finding the range

Results of a science exam taken in Year 6:

65, 72, 32, 89, 78, 56, 61

The smallest number is 32.

The largest number is 89.

The range is the difference between 89 and 32.

The range is 57.

DEVELOP

Below are the marks awarded for a mental arithmetic test out of 25.

11, 8, 20, 14, 17, 20

① What is the mode?

② What is the mean?

③ What is the range?

④ What is the median?

TIMED TEST 12

① Ankush enjoys running and he keeps a diary of his distances covered. These are the distances over a six-week period.

4.5 km   3.5 km   5 km   6.5 km   4.5 km   6 km

What is the mean distance travelled per week?

A	**B**	**C**	**D**	**E**
5.5 km	6 km	7.5 km	6.5 km	5 km

② In a kitchen cupboard the following volumes were recorded on different food cans and bottles.

650 ml   800 ml   300 ml   200 ml   50 ml

What is the mean?

A	**B**	**C**	**D**	**E**
500 ml	200 ml	300 ml	400 ml	150 ml

③ The masses of John's pets are listed below.

20 kg   8 kg   200 g   800 g   1 kg   6 kg

What is the mean?

A	**B**	**C**	**D**	**E**
6 kg	5 kg	700 g	8 kg	900 g

④ A shop sells 14 blue, 32 green, 12 white, 47 black and 17 red coats. What is the median?

A	**B**	**C**	**D**	**E**
47	32	14	12	17

⑤ Oli received the following amounts of pocket money for helping around the house.

£2.80   £3.25   £2.50   £4.75   £1.25

What is the range?

A	**B**	**C**	**D**	**E**
£3.25	£4.00	£3.50	£4.25	£4.50

⑥ Five television programmes last for different lengths of time.

35 minutes   45 minutes   90 minutes   60 minutes   30 minutes

What is the mean?

A	**B**	**C**	**D**	**E**
62 minutes	56 minutes	52 minutes	60 minutes	30 minutes

⑦ In a shop, some biscuits cost the following amounts.

£4.24   £3.99   £1.98   £1.79   £3

What is the mean?

A	**B**	**C**	**D**	**E**
£3	£4	£5.50	£6.50	£3.99

⑧ What is the median from the five buildings in a high street that measure the following?

| 1050 ft | 980 ft | 1020 ft | 870 ft | 1010 ft |

A	**B**	**C**	**D**	**E**
980 ft	1050 ft	1020 ft	1010 ft	870 ft

⑨ The following number of tickets were sold for different days of a pop concert:

| 20 000 | 35 000 | 25 000 | 39 000 | 31 000 |

What is the mean?

A	**B**	**C**	**D**	**E**
40 000	25 000	30 000	45 000	20 000

⑩ On five separate days in London, the temperatures were:

| −2°C | 10°C | 21°C | −7°C | 11°C |

What is the range?

A	**B**	**C**	**D**	**E**
8°C	28°C	17°C	12°C	18°C

⑪ The total mass of seven rugby players is 630 kg. What is their mean mass?

A	**B**	**C**	**D**	**E**
100 kg	70 kg	90 kg	110 kg	80 kg

⑫ A diver recorded these water temperatures in degrees Celsius:
8, −7, 5, −5, 6, −1, 0, 2, 6, 8, 8, 9
What is the median?

A	**B**	**C**	**D**	**E**
5	5.5	6	7	4

⑬ What is the mean of the following numbers? 227, 103, 258, 386, 441

A	**B**	**C**	**D**	**E**
227	238	258	283	328

⑭ Jane spent the following amounts in her local post office: £3.02, £5.76, £4.43, £5.23, £6.70, £1.39. What is the range?

A	**B**	**C**	**D**	**E**
£5.31	£5.21	£5.41	£5.32	£5.33

⑮ The mean of five numbers is 180. Four of the numbers are 155, 162, 190 and 198. What is the fifth number?

A	**B**	**C**	**D**	**E**
190	180	175	195	185

Lesson 18: Conversion

LEARN

In this topic you will learn about **converting units of measurement and units of time**. Conversion is a topic that can cause confusion. It is a topic which often appears in maths exams as well as in everyday life, so it is important that you can convert confidently.

Conversion of units of measurement

There are two systems of measurement which continue to be used. They are:

1) The metric system, which is most commonly used in the UK and other parts of Europe
2) The imperial system, which is more traditional, is mainly used in parts of Africa, Asia and America as well as in some situations in the UK (e.g. road signs).

Tables 1 and 2 show the different units of mass (weight), length (distance) and volume (capacity) and Table 3 shows a comparison of both.

Table 1: Metric system

Length	Weight	Capacity
10 mm = 1 cm	1000 mg = 1 g	1000 ml = 1 litre
100 cm = 1 m	1000 g = 1 kg	100 cl = 1 litre
1000 m = 1 km	1000 kg = 1 tonne	1000 cm³ = 1 litre

Table 2: Imperial system

12 inches =	1 foot
3 feet =	1 yard
16 ounces =	1 pound
14 pounds =	1 stone
8 pints =	1 gallon
$\frac{2}{5}$ hectare =	1 acre

Table 3: Metric units to imperial units (approx.)

0.91 m =	1 yard
1.6 km =	1 mile
1 m =	39 inches
30 cm =	1 foot
2.5 cm =	1 inch
1 kg =	2.2 pounds
28 g =	1 ounce
1 litre =	1.75 pints
4.5 litres =	1 gallon

LEARN

Time conversion

It is also important to have a good knowledge of how to convert between different *time* periods. Below is a table to help you.

Table 4

60 seconds =	1 minute
60 minutes =	1 hour
24 hours =	1 day
7 days =	1 week
52 weeks =	1 year
12 months =	1 year
10 years =	1 decade
100 years =	1 century

'k' refers to kilo, which is associated with 1000. 'c' refers to cent, which is associated with 100.

How to apply conversion to the metric system

It is important to know how to multiply and divide by 10, 100 and 1000 because, in the metric system, the units are related to their sub-units (e.g. km to m to cm to mm) by powers of 10. More information on powers of 10 can be found in Lesson 7 on page 38.

If you are converting from a large known unit to a smaller unit, you have to multiply. For example, 3 kilometres converted to metres is 3000 metres.

If you are converting from a small known unit to a large unit, you have to divide. For example, 2000 grams converted to kilograms is 2 kilograms.

kg to g	convert		inverse		
3 kg	3 × 1000	3000 g	3000 g	3000 ÷ 1000	3 kg
km to m					
2 km	2 × 1000	2000 m	2000 m	2000 ÷ 1000	2 km
L to ml					
4 L	4 × 1000	4000 ml	4000 ml	4000 ÷ 1000	4 L
m to cm					
8 m	8 × 100	800 cm	800 cm	800 ÷ 100	8 m
cm to mm					
5 cm	5 × 10	50 mm	50 mm	50 ÷ 10	5 cm

To convert 5 cm to mm: 5 × 10 = 50 mm

Use the inverse to convert 50 mm to cm: 50 ÷ 10 = 5 cm

DEVELOP

Metric conversion

① Convert 384 m to centimetres.

② How many kilograms are in 9800 g?

③ Convert 27 300 ml to litres.

④ How many centimetres are in 8 m?

⑤ Convert 98 cm to millimetres.

⑥ How many metres in 9.7 km?

⑦ Convert 0.7 L to millilitres.

⑧ How many grams are in 0.07 kg?

⑨ Convert 420 mm to centimetres.

⑩ How many millimetres are in 7 m?

Time conversion

⑪ Convert 9 years to months.

⑫ How many years are in 18 centuries?

⑬ Convert 1440 seconds to minutes.

⑭ How many years are in 12 decades?

⑮ How many years equates to 7 millennia?

⑯ Convert 7 hours to minutes.

⑰ How many seconds are in 10 hours?

⑱ Convert the month of July to hours.

⑲ How many seconds is 3.5 hours?

⑳ Convert 8 years to days.

TIMED TEST 13

① A glass holds 50 ml of juice. How many glasses can Jovan fill from six 1-litre bottles?

A	B	C	D	E
80	120	20	60	12

② It took Lara three weeks to complete her history project. She worked on it for four hours a night. How many minutes, in total, did it take her to complete the project?

A	B	C	D	E
4050 mins	5000 mins	84 mins	3000 mins	5040 mins

③ The average length of a car is 3.5 metres. If there are 3000 cars in a bumper-to-bumper traffic jam, determine the length of the queue in kilometres.

A	B	C	D	E
10.5 km	10 km	15 km	300 km	35 km

④ Jess and Neil are celebrating their silver wedding anniversary this year. This is equivalent to 25 full years of marriage. On the actual time of their anniversary, how many hours would they have they been married?

A	B	C	D	E
91 250 h	190 000 h	219 144 h	9125 h	219 000 h

⑤ There is a cycling competition organised between schools in Year 6. Pinak decides to enter. He travels 4 metres every second. How far will he travel, in kilometres, in 20 minutes?

A	B	C	D	E
2.4 km	24 km	3 km	4.2 km	4.8 km

⑥ It took a total of three and a half full days to prepare for John and Myra's diamond wedding banquet. How many minutes, in total, was this?

A	B	C	D	E
5040 mins	84 mins	3500 mins	5300 mins	405 mins

⑦ Sam bought 10 tins of nails which come in one box. The box weighed 15 kg. What is the mass, in grams, of each tin of nails?

A	B	C	D	E
1000 g	1500 g	1.5 g	15 g	15 000 g

⑧ Helen decides to enter for a junior triathlon. She has to run for 240 000 cm, swim for 800 m and cycle for 3.5 km. What is the total distance, in kilometres, Helen has to cover?

A	B	C	D	E
6.9 km	6.53 km	6.7 km	65 km	6.5 km

⑨ It is Wednesday, and Ishleen attends the lunch-time science club. The topic today is dissolving salt. The teacher divides four 1.5 kg bags of salt evenly between 15 club members. How many kilograms has Ishleen been given?

A	**B**	**C**	**D**	**E**
0.4 kg	0.5 kg	40 kg	4 kg	5 kg

⑩ Krish was decorating his bedroom. In total he used 4.75 litres of paint. How many millilitres did he use?

A	**B**	**C**	**D**	**E**
4570 ml	4750 ml	475 ml	457 ml	45.7 ml

⑪ It took Kevin 25 minutes to walk home from school. How long did it take him in seconds?

A	**B**	**C**	**D**	**E**
15 000	180	1500	150	1800

⑫ Neil bought four 17 kg bags of dog food on a special promotion for his two dogs. How many grams of food did he buy?

A	**B**	**C**	**D**	**E**
6800 g	17 000 g	6500 g	68 000 g	12 000 g

⑬ In Miriam's maths lesson, she was taught how to convert imperial measurement to metric. At school, she measures the distance from her classroom to the dining hall as 236 yards. If 1 yard is equal to 0.91 metres, what is the distance in metres?

A	**B**	**C**	**D**	**E**
217.64 m	214.76 m	387.95 m	236.09 m	91.23 m

⑭ Trevor filled his car with 15 gallons of petrol. It cost him £1.08 per litre. If the conversion rate is 1 gallon to 4.5 litres, how much did it cost in pounds for Trevor to fill his car?

A	**B**	**C**	**D**	**E**
£79.20	£72.09	£67.50	£72.90	£21.48

⑮ James's school field has an area of 15 acres. His task was to find the conversion rate from acres to hectares and tell the class the equivalent size of the field, in hectares. He read that 1 acre is equal to $\frac{2}{5}$ hectare. How many hectares is the area of James's school field?

A	**B**	**C**	**D**	**E**
9	3	7	8	6

THIS PAGE HAS DELIBERATELY BEEN LEFT BLANK

SECTION 5:

DATA HANDLING AND INTERPRETATION

Lesson 19: Bar Charts

LEARN

Data is information that can be collected and illustrated ('handled') in some way such as on a line graph, bar chart or pie chart.

By analysing the graph or the chart, conclusions or 'interpretations' can be made about the data. When presented with data questions in the 11+ exam, it is important to read the information as accurately as possible to make sure you answer correctly.

How would you, or other people in your class, answer these questions?

- How many brothers or sisters do you have?
- How do you travel to school?
- What pets do you have?
- What is your favourite colour?

Such individual answers may be interesting to know but it would be far more interesting to compare your answers with everyone else's in the class. This would enable you to make comparisons and draw conclusions from the data collected. For example, a dog may be the most common pet or blue may be the most popular colour.

In the 11+ exams, you would normally be asked to interpret the information shown rather than be asked to construct a graph (mainly due to limited time).

LEARN

There are two types of data:

Discrete data (or grouped) data refers to data that can be counted. The data includes values that are distinct or separate, such as the number of puppies in a litter. This information is often shown in the form of a bar chart or pie chart.

Continuous data is data that is obtained by measuring. It can take on any value, such as temperature, mass, height and rainfall. Such data is often shown in the form of a line graph.

Bar charts
A bar chart is often used to compare numbers, or frequency, of occurrences. It can be used to show both discrete and continuous data. It is made up of bars or columns of equal width. The bars are normally drawn with gaps between them and their height shows the frequency of occurrences.

Example one: Bar charts and frequency charts
Now we will go through the process of drawing a bar chart from discrete data that has been tabulated in a **frequency chart** (Table 1).

Table 1: A frequency chart to show the number of house points collected in the autumn term by Year 6 children

Number of house points	Number of children (frequency)
1–10	8
11–20	12
21–30	33
31–40	28
41–50	10

From Table 1 you can see the groups are separated (1 to 10, 11 to 20, etc).

If you are asked to draw a bar chart, you don't need to add up all the children. Instead look at the highest number in the frequency column. In this example it is 33 children. Then decide on the intervals for the vertical axis of the bar chart. These have to be equal intervals so that the length of the bar can be used to represent the frequency. Then draw on the bars for each of the frequency columns.

LEARN

Bar chart 1: Illustrating Table 1 data

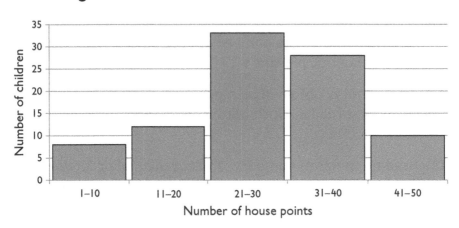

Example two: Bar charts with continuous data and tally charts

Now let's look at drawing a bar chart with continuous data tabulated in a **tally chart** (Table 2).

Table 2: A tally chart to show the amount of money raised in a sponsored readathon by Year 5 children.

Money raised (£)	Number of children	Frequency
$0 \leq x < 10$	﹢﹢﹢ ﹢﹢﹢	10
$10 \leq x < 20$	﹢﹢﹢ ﹢﹢﹢ ﹢﹢﹢ ﹢﹢﹢ ﹢﹢﹢	25
$20 \leq x < 30$	﹢﹢﹢ ﹢﹢﹢ ﹢﹢﹢ ﹢﹢﹢ ﹢﹢﹢ |||	28
$30 \leq x < 40$	﹢﹢﹢ ﹢﹢﹢ |||	13
$40 \leq x < 50$	﹢﹢﹢ ﹢﹢﹢ ﹢﹢﹢	15

In Table 2 you can see that the groups are continuous, as shown in the money column.

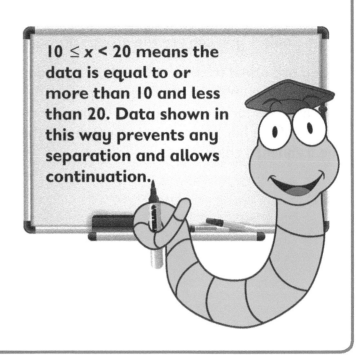

$10 \leq x < 20$ means the data is equal to or more than 10 and less than 20. Data shown in this way prevents any separation and allows continuation.

LEARN

Bar chart 2: Illustrating Table 2 data

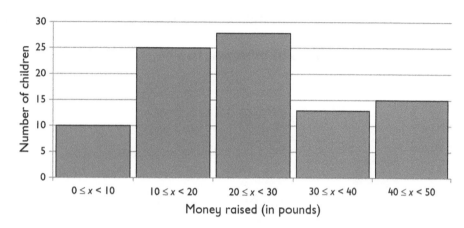

There are also other types of bar charts about which you may need to answer questions in the exam or everyday life, so it is good to be able to recognise as many as possible.

A = Comparative, or dual bar chart
B = Horizontal bar chart
C = Standard bar chart
D = Composite bar chart – demonstrates multiple data points
E = 3D horizontal bar chart

A

B

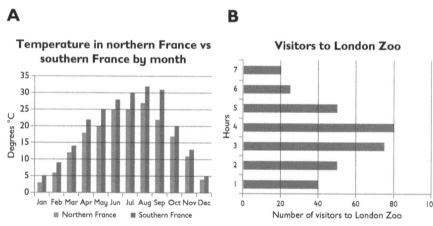

C   **D**   **E**

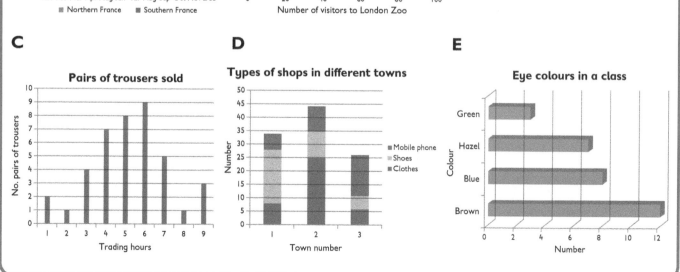

DEVELOP

See if you can answer the questions below.

Look at the composite (stacked) bar chart below and answer the following questions:

Types of shops in different towns

Legend:
- Mobile phone
- Shoes
- Clothes

(Y-axis: Number, from 0 to 50; X-axis: Town number, 1, 2, 3)

① How many shops in total were surveyed?

② How many mobile phone shops in total were there?

③ Which town has the least number of shoe shops?

④ How many more shoe shops are in town 1 than in town 3?

⑤ Work out the combined number of shoe shops and clothes shops in towns 2 and 3.

Lesson 20: Line Graphs

LEARN

A line graph shows **a line joining a set of points**. The points represent the relationship between two variables, such as distance and time.

Line graphs normally display **continuous data**, and have a vertical and a horizontal axis. This line graph shows the daily hours of sunshine in a week, with the 'number of hours of sunshine' on the vertical axis and the 'days of the week' on the horizontal axis.

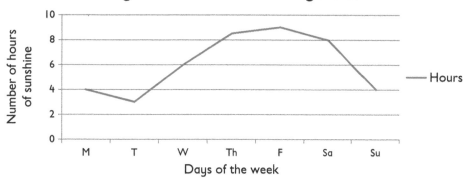

There are also other types of line graph, including horizontal and vertical bar line charts. On the next page are some more examples.

LEARN

A

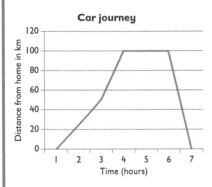

Car journey

B

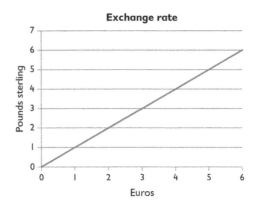

Exchange rate

C

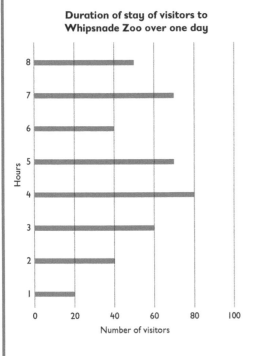

Duration of stay of visitors to Whipsnade Zoo over one day

D

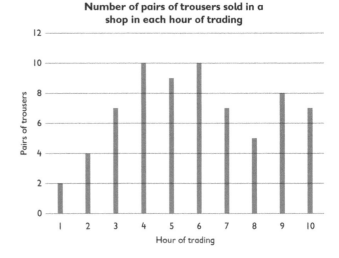

Number of pairs of trousers sold in a shop in each hour of trading

A   Journey tracking chart

B   Conversion chart

C   Horizontal bar line chart

D   Vertical bar line chart

DEVELOP

Answer the following questions about the line graph below.

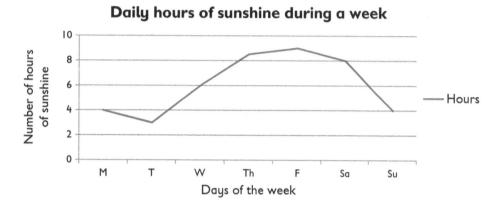

Daily hours of sunshine during a week

(1) On which day were the most hours of sunshine recorded?

(2) Which two days had the same number of sunshine hours?

(3) Which day had the least number of hours of sunshine?

(4) What was the total number of hours of sunshine in the week?

(5) What was the range in hours of sunshine during the week?

To find the number of hours, read up to the line directly above the letter of the day of the week.

Lesson 21: Pie Charts, Pictograms and Venn Diagrams

LEARN

As well as bar charts and line graphs, there are a number of other ways to display data visually, for example pie charts, pictograms and Venn diagrams. They can display different sets of data in different ways and in this lesson you will see some examples.

Pie charts: In a pie chart, all (100%) of the data is shown in a circle (360°) that is split into sections. Each section represents a numerical proportion. A pie chart is a good way to show relative sizes of data and each 'slice of the pie' may be labelled with its percentage value.

Pictogram: A pictogram is a chart that uses pictures or symbols to represent a certain number of items. Each symbol has to be the same size with equal gaps between them. Each row should be labelled and a key given.

Venn diagrams: A Venn diagram is a diagram in which data sets and their relationships are represented by circles. The sets of data usually have something in common and this is where the circles overlap.

An example of each is shown on the following pages.

It is important to remember that 360° in a pie chart equals 100%.

DEVELOP

See if you can answer the following questions about the pie chart, pictogram and Venn diagram.

Pie chart: The favourite colours of 600 children

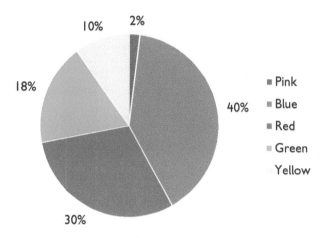

① How many children preferred the colour red?

② What was the percentage of children whose favourite colour was blue?

③ What was the angle of the pie slice made up of the children whose favourite colour was yellow?

④ What was the total number of children who preferred blue and pink?

⑤ How many more children liked red than yellow?

Pictogram: Children's favourite television programmes

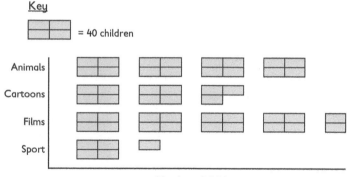

⑥ How many children preferred animal programmes?

⑦ How many more children preferred to watch films than cartoons?

⑧ How many children altogether preferred to watch films and sport?

⑨ What was the least popular type of programme?

⑩ What was the difference between the most and least popular type of programme?

DEVELOP

Venn diagram: Children's pets in Class 6A

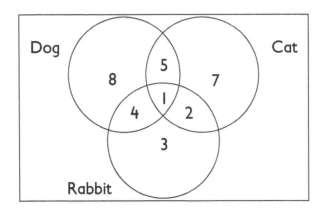

⑪ How many children have a dog and a rabbit but not a cat?

⑫ How many children have all types of animals?

⑬ How many children have a cat and a dog but not a rabbit?

⑭ How many children are in the class?

⑮ How many children have either a cat or a rabbit only?

A Venn diagram is useful because it shows relationships between different pieces of information.

TIMED TEST 14

 15:00
15 minutes

Look at the **comparative dual bar chart** below and answer the following questions.

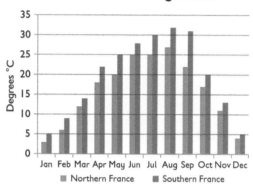

Temperature in northern France vs southern France by month

① Which is the warmest month to live in southern France?

A	**B**	**C**	**D**	**E**
Oct	June	Aug	Sept	May

② Which two months have same temperature in northern France?

A	**B**	**C**	**D**	**E**
Jun & Jul	Jan & Dec	Oct & May	Jul & Sept	May & Oct

③ In which month was the lowest recorded temperature in northern France?

A	**B**	**C**	**D**	**E**
Aug	Jan	Dec	Sept	Feb

④ What is the range of temperatures in southern France?

A	**B**	**C**	**D**	**E**
20 degrees	21 degrees	24 degrees	28 degrees	27 degrees

A bar chart is a good way to compare lots of information.

This **conversion chart** is used to convert amounts of money between pounds and euros. Answer the following questions using the graph.

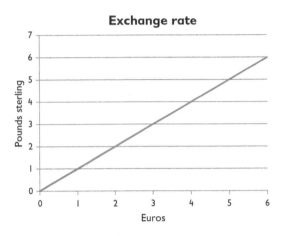

Exchange rate

5 Convert 5 euros to the nearest pound.

A	B	C	D	E
£2	£5	£2.50	£4	£3.10

6 How many euros is £6?

A	B	C	D	E
6 euros	7 euros	9 euros	7.5 euros	8.5 euros

7 On holiday in France, a taxi ride cost 15 euros. How much is this in pounds?

A	B	C	D	E
£15	£10	£20	£9	£8

Now answer the following questions about the **pie chart** below.

Top five hobbies

Key	
Football	
Reading	
Computer games	
Dance	
Cooking	

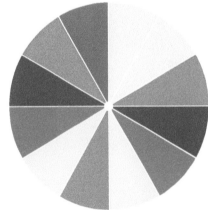

⑧ What is the total angle representing dance on the pie chart?

A	B	C	D	E
30°	90°	25°	60°	50°

⑨ If 60 children liked reading the most, how many children altogether liked computer games and football the most?

A	B	C	D	E
300	210	360	270	420

⑩ What fraction of the children in the survey favoured dance? In its simplest form the fraction is:

A	B	C	D	E
$\frac{2}{12}$	$\frac{1}{4}$	$\frac{2}{6}$	$\frac{1}{6}$	$\frac{1}{3}$

⑪ What percentage of children's favourite hobby was computer games?

A	B	C	D	E
40%	25%	36%	20%	30%

The **pictogram** below shows the types of litter collected in a park in 1 day.

Crisp packets	CRISPS	CRISPS	CRISPS	CRISPS	CRIS
Cans	🥫	🥫	🥫		
Bottles	🍾	🍾	🍾	🍾	🍾

Key 🍟 = 100 crisp packets   🥫 = 100 cans   🍾 = 100 bottles

⑫ How many bottles were collected in total during the day?

A	B	C	D	E
100	700	500	400	450

⑬ How many more crisp packets than cans were collected?

A	B	C	D	E
150	25	100	125	50

⑭ How many crisp packets and cans were collected in total?

A	B	C	D	E
675	725	700	750	650

⑮ How many items of rubbish were collected in total?

A	B	C	D	E
900	1150	1000	800	1100

**THIS PAGE HAS DELIBERATELY
BEEN LEFT BLANK**

SECTION 6:

SHAPE AND SPACE

LEARN

Types of angles

In the CEM 11+ exams, you will not have any mathematical equipment. Therefore, it is important that you can recognise the main angles as you are unable to use a protractor to measure them. The size of the turn determines the type of angle. Below are some examples of these angles.

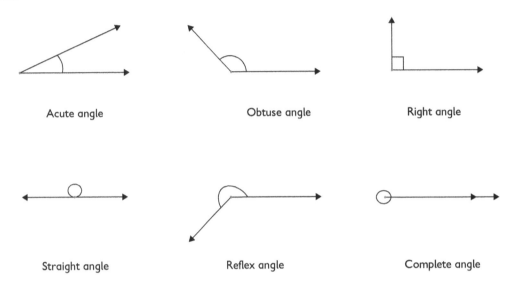

Before doing your exam, it is a good idea to learn the main angle names. For example, a question might be, 'What is the name for an angle of 112°?'

An angle less than (<) 90° is called acute.
An angle more than (>) 90° but less than (<) 180° is called an obtuse angle.
An angle greater than (>) 180° is called a reflex angle.
An angle of 90° is called a right angle.
Two angles that add up to 180° are called supplementary.
Two angles that add up to 90° are called complementary.

An angle of 112° is between 90° and 180° so is called obtuse.

Interior angles

The other important facts to remember when learning about angles are the interior angles of different shapes. A very useful formula to help you work out any shape's interior angles is shown below:

$(n - 2) \times 180$ = interior angles of the shape

n = number of sides of the shape

LEARN

Example one: Working out the interior angles of a shape

So, if we have a quadrilateral (four-sided shape) we can substitute the *n* for 4.

$(4 - 2) \times 180 = 360°$

Missing angles

Using simple algebraic equations can help you to work out unknown angles in shapes.

Example two: Working out the missing angle in a triangle

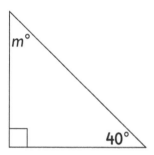

Find the total of the interior angles of a triangle (a three-sided shape) by using the formula previously given: $(3 - 2) \times 180 = 180°$, so the angles of a triangle add up to 180°. By writing out the question as a simple algebraic equation, we can find the missing angle, *m*°.

$m° = 180 - (90° + 40°)$

$m° = 180 - 130$

$m° = 50$

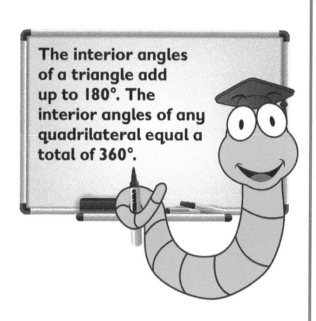

The interior angles of a triangle add up to 180°. The interior angles of any quadrilateral equal a total of 360°.

DEVELOP

Try the questions below to see how much you know about angles.

① What type of angle is an angle that is 185°?

② How many degrees are there between 12 o'clock and 3 o'clock on a clock face? And what is this angle called?

③ What type of angle is an angle that is 30°?

④ In a regular pentagon, what is the total of the interior angles?

⑤ What type of angle is an angle that is 164°?

⑥ In a supplementary angle, one angle is 17°. What is the other one?

⑦ In this triangle, how many degrees is angle A°?

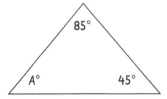

⑧ What is the value of Q°?

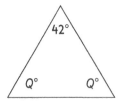

⑨ Can you work out the value of P° in the circle below?

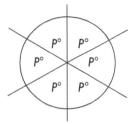

⑩ What are the angles A° and B°?

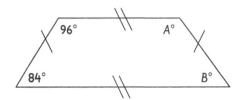

TIMED TEST 15

 15:00 15 minutes

① Two angles on a straight line are 130° and 19°. What is the size of the third angle?

A	**B**	**C**	**D**	**E**
31°	180°	39°	90°	50°

② A ship was facing south west and turned the bow 270° anti-clockwise. Which way is the ship facing now?

A	**B**	**C**	**D**	**E**
west	south	south east	north east	north west

③ A shape has eight regular sides. How many degrees is each individual interior angle?

A	**B**	**C**	**D**	**E**
360°	135°	10°	45°	18°

④ If Zak faces north west and turns 135° clockwise, which way will he be facing?

A	**B**	**C**	**D**	**E**
south	west	south east	east	north east

⑤ Inside a scalene triangle two of the angles are 21° and 67°. What is the size of the third angle?

A	**B**	**C**	**D**	**E**
180°	80°	90°	35°	92°

⑥ How many sides does a shape with interior angles totalling 1440° have?

A	**B**	**C**	**D**	**E**
14	6	12	8	10

⑦ How many degrees are between 10 o'clock and 2 o'clock on a clock face?

A	**B**	**C**	**D**	**E**
180°	150°	120°	140°	110°

⑧ The top angle of an isosceles triangle is 40°. What is the size of one of the base angles?

A	**B**	**C**	**D**	**E**
50°	80°	70°	140°	90°

⑨ In the pentagon below, what is the value of M°?

A	B	C	D	E
130°	120°	50°	145°	135°

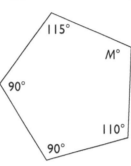

⑩ What is the value of x°?

A	B	C	D	E
79°	69°	111°	159°	175°

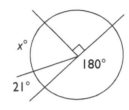

⑪ Which of the following is a reflex angle?

A	B	C	D	E
79°	37°	202°	179°	150°

⑫ One angle measures 35°. What is its supplementary angle?

A	B	C	D	E
325°	145°	55°	100°	155°

⑬ A boat turns its rudder 55°. What would be its complementary angle?

A	B	C	D	E
100°	45°	90°	35°	145°

⑭ Inside a kite there are three angles measuring 95°, 95° and 58°. What is the fourth angle?

A	B	C	D	E
125°	115°	95°	114°	112°

⑮ A car windscreen is the shape of a trapezium. It has two angles of 72°. What are the other two angles combined?

A	B	C	D	E
90°	216°	218°	72°	145°

LEARN

In the 11+ exams you may be asked questions about 2D shapes. 2D shapes are sometimes called **polygons**. All the sides of a regular polygon are the same length and all the angles are equal. All other polygons are irregular. It is important to be able to recognise the common 2D shapes and also know their **properties**.

Below are some pictures of common 2D shapes. Can you match the names to the shapes?

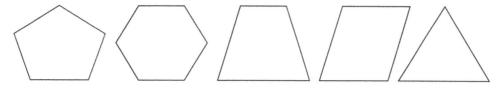

hexagon   trapezium   rhombus   triangle   pentagon

We are surrounded by shapes in everyday life, for example different shaped windows, and it can be fun exploring their properties, such as how many right angles are inside your front door. When describing shapes, we often use the following words: vertices, pairs of parallel sides, perpendicular sides and angles.

This table shows the properties of some 2D shapes.

Name of shape	Vertices (corners)	Pairs of parallel sides	Perpendicular sides
square	4	2	2
rectangle	4	2	2
trapezium	4	1	0
kite	4	0	0
oval (ellipse)	0	0	0
regular pentagon	5	0	0
regular hexagon	6	3	0

DEVELOP

All the following questions relate to 2D shapes.

①   How many sides does an ellipse have?

②   How many sides does a parallelogram have?

③   Can you name five quadrilaterals?

    (i)

    (ii)

    (iii)

    (iv)

    (v)

④   A 50 p coin is based on which polygon?

⑤   Which of the following shapes is irregular?

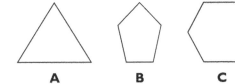

    A   **B**   **C**   **D**

⑥   How many pairs of parallel sides does a parallelogram have?

⑦   How many equal sides does a rhombus have?

⑧   How many sides does a decagon have?

⑨   What is a nine-sided shape called?

⑩   What type of shape is this?

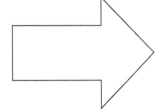

Lesson 24: 3D Shapes

LEARN

Recognising 3D shapes and being able to name them is important. Can you name this common 3D shape?

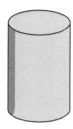

When describing 3D shapes, you must use the correct terminology. Use the diagram and definitions below to help you understand the terms.

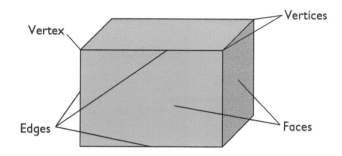

Vertices (singular: vertex)   points or corners on a solid 3D shape.

Edges   where two faces meet on a solid 3D shape.

Faces   the flat parts on a solid 3D shape.

Being able to recognise the features of any 3D shape is important.

DEVELOP

Now try to answer these questions about 3D shapes.

① How many vertices does a triangular prism have?

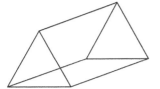

② How many faces does a cylinder have?

③ What is the total number of edges of a cube and cuboid added together?

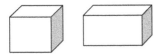

④ How many faces does a tetrahedron have?

⑤ Total the number of vertices of a pentagonal prism and a square-based pyramid.

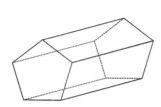 

⑥ Multiply the vertices on a sphere by the faces on a hexagonal prism.

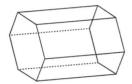

DEVELOP

⑦ How many faces does a cone have?

⑧ How many faces does a dodecahedron have?

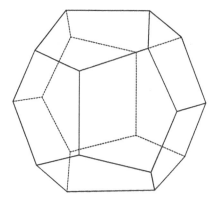

⑨ How many edges does a square-based pyramid have?

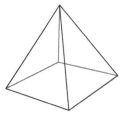

⑩ What is the name of a 3D shape that has two edges, three faces and no vertices?

TIMED TEST 16

15:00
15 minutes

① Which of the following pairs of lines are parallel?

A   **B**   **C**   **D**

② What is the sum of the sides of a nonagon and decagon?

A	**B**	**C**	**D**
11	18	19	21

③ A triangle has angles 95°, 11° and 74°. What is the name of this type of triangle?

A	**B**	**C**	**D**
isosceles	scalene	right angled	equilateral

④ What is the order of rotational symmetry of a square?

A	**B**	**C**	**D**
1	4	3	8

⑤ Can you complete the following passage using the words from the table?

equal	rectangle	ninety	diagonals	sides	parallel	two

A ……………... has ……… pairs of equal ………. The angles are all ……… and the

…………. are equal. Each angle is …………… degrees. This shape is sometimes called

an oblong. It has two pairs of …………… sides.

⑥ Multiply the number of vertices a heptagon has by the number of edges an octagon has.

A	**B**	**C**	**D**
63	54	56	64

⑦ Which shape is a quadrilateral?

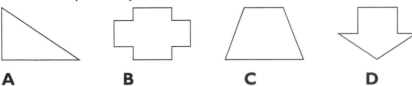

A   **B**   **C**   **D**

⑧ Divide the number of sides a nonagon has by the number of sides a scalene triangle has.

A	B	C	D
2	6	9	3

⑨ Which of the following shapes has eight sides?

A	B	C	D

⑩ Which of the following pairs of lines are perpendicular?

A	B	C	D

⑪ Zoe has a cuboid-shaped box of chocolates. What is the total of its faces and vertices?

A	B	C	D	E
14	10	16	8	20

⑫ John's pencil holder on his desk is a hexagonal prism. How many vertices does it have?

A	B	C	D	E
10	16	5	12	4

⑬ Multiply the number of faces a cone has by the number of faces a triangular prism has.

A	B	C	D	E
3	10	6	14	8

⑭ What is the name of this shape when the net is folded up?

A	B	C	D
hemisphere	sphere	cube	square-based pyramid

⑮ How many hemispheres are required to make six spheres?

A	B	C	D	E
2	24	12	6	8

Lesson 25: Perimeter and Area

LEARN

The key words perimeter and area can often be forgotten or muddled up. Let's make sure you've remembered the difference between these measurements.

Perimeter: This is the total distance around the edge of a 2D shape. It can be measured in mm, cm, m or km.

Area: This is the space inside the perimeter and can be counted in square units. It can be measured in mm^2, cm^2, m^2 or km^2.

Example one: Finding the perimeter of a 2D shape

To find the perimeter of a 2D shape, you must add together all the side lengths. Below is a diagram which shows how to calculate the perimeter.

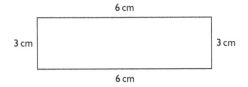

Perimeter = 6 cm + 3 cm + 6 cm + 3 cm = 18 cm

Using a dot or eliminating each line as the sides are added together can help to avoid missing one out or counting one again.

When calculating the perimeter of a rectangle, you can use the following formula:

P = 2(L + W)

***P* is the perimeter, *L* is the length and *W* is the width of the rectangle.**

Example two: Finding the area of a 2D shape

To find the area of a 2D shape, you multiply the sides together. So, if a square has sides of 7 cm, you can simply multiply 7 cm by 7 cm to give $49\,cm^2$. A simple formula can also be written to find the area of a rectangle.

A = L × W

***A* is the area, *L* is the length and *W* is the width of the rectangle.**

Here is another example:

	1	2	3	4	5	6	7	8
	9	10	11	12	13	14	15	16

2 cm

8 cm

$A = 8\,cm × 2\,cm = 16\,cm^2$

LEARN

Below are the formulae for finding the areas of triangles, parallelograms and trapeziums. As for tasks involving angles, you can use simple algebraic expressions to help answer questions on shapes.

Triangle: $A = \frac{1}{2}$ base × height

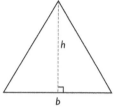

Parallelogram: $A =$ base × height

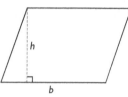

Trapezium: $A = \frac{1}{2}(a + b)h$

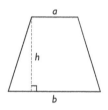

DEVELOP

①   What is the perimeter of a rectangle that measures 6 m by 2 m?

②   Find the area of a square with side length 9 cm.

③   The total perimeter of a square is 28 cm. What is the length of one side?

④   Calculate the area of a rectangle with a length of 15 cm and a width of 6 cm.

⑤   If a regular hexagon has sides of 8 cm, what is the perimeter?

⑥   Find the perimeter of this triangle.

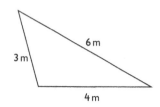

DEVELOP

⑦ What is the area of this triangle?

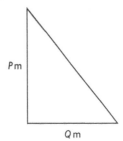

Pm

Qm

⑧ If the side of a regular hexagon is w and the perimeter is 48 cm, what is the value of w?

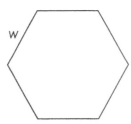

W

⑨ The area of this rectangle is 50 cm², so what is the value of l?

2 cm

l

⑩ The area of this square is 9 cm², so what is the value of t?

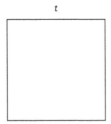

t

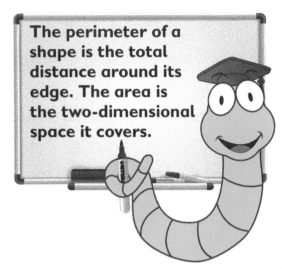

The perimeter of a shape is the total distance around its edge. The area is the two-dimensional space it covers.

TIMED TEST 17

① Find the area of a square whose perimeter is 24 cm.

A	**B**	**C**	**D**	**E**
72 cm²	64 cm²	16 cm²	36 cm²	48 cm²

② If the area of a rectangle is 60 cm² and the length is 10 cm, what is the width?

A	**B**	**C**	**D**	**E**
6 cm	10 cm	12 cm	4 cm	8 cm

③ What is the perimeter of a rectangle with a width of 7 cm and a length of 11 cm?

A	**B**	**C**	**D**	**E**
28 cm	36 cm	44 cm	50 cm	77 cm

④ What is the area of a square with sides of length 12 m?

A	**B**	**C**	**D**	**E**
136 m²	168 m²	140 m²	144 m²	150 m²

⑤ What is the perimeter of a regular heptagon that has sides 9 cm long?

A	**B**	**C**	**D**	**E**
72 cm	54 cm	80 cm	63 cm	60 cm

⑥ Find the perimeter of this triangle.

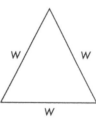

A	**B**	**C**	**D**	**E**
w^3	$3w + w$	$w + w + w$	w^2	$w + w$

⑦ What is the area of this triangle?

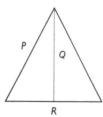

A	**B**	**C**	**D**	**E**
$R + Q$	QR	$(\frac{1}{2}R)Q$	$(\frac{1}{2}Q)P$	$\frac{1}{2}PR$

⑧ If *w* is 4 cm, what is the area?

A	B	C	D	E
16 cm²	32 cm²	38 cm²	24 cm²	30 cm²

8 cm

w

⑨ If the area is 100 cm², what is the value of *l*?

A	B	C	D	E
40 cm	10 cm	20 cm	45 cm	15 cm

5 cm

l

⑩ If the area of the triangle is 25 cm², what is the value of *x*?

A	B	C	D	E
5 cm	18 cm	20 cm	12 cm	10 cm

5 cm

x

⑪ An ant walks all the way around the edge of a rectangular patio tile. If the tile measures 0.6 m by 1.2 m, how far does the ant walk in centimetres?

A	B	C	D	E
3.6 m	300 cm	1.8 m	360 cm	180 cm

⑫ A flower bed has a total perimeter of 24 metres. If the length is 8 m, what is the length of the two widths together?

A	B	C	D	E
2 m	16 m	18 m	4 m	8 m

⑬ A luggage tag had edges of 6 cm and 3.5 cm. What is the area of the tag in square millimetres?

A	B	C	D	E
200 mm²	19.5 mm²	180 mm²	2100 mm²	1950 mm²

⑭ The side window of a car was a parallelogram in shape. If the base was 0.5 m long and the height was 0.4 m, what was the area in square metres?

A	B	C	D	E
2 m²	0.2 m²	1 m²	0.4 m²	4 m²

⑮ Amy has a rectangular rose garden that measures 8 m by 12.5 m. One bag of fertilizer can cover 16 m². How many bags will she need to cover the rose garden?

A	B	C	D	E
8	3	5	7	9

LEARN

Volume

The volume of a solid 3D object is the amount of space it takes up. Volume can be measured in mm^3, cm^3 or m^3. To find the volume of a cube or cuboid, you multiply together the length (L), width (W) and height (H). This can be represented as $L \times W \times H$.

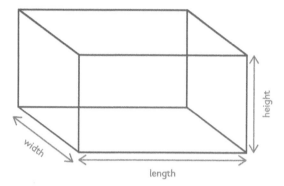

Therefore, to calculate the volume of a cuboid that is 9 cm in length, 5 cm in width and 8 cm in height, use $L \times W \times H$.

9 cm × 5 cm × 8 cm = 360 cm^3

Capacity

The capacity is the amount of liquid or water a container can hold. You measure capacity in litres (L) or millilitres (ml).

To help solve capacity questions, it is useful to know simple equivalent values. Can you complete the table below? Lesson 18 also helps you with conversions.

Container	Litres	Millilitres
Bucket	8 L	
Bottle of juice	1 L	
Water bottle	0.5 L	
Mug of coffee	0.3 L	
Cup of tea	0.2 L	
1 teaspoon of medicine	0.025 L	

Another important measure of capacity is centilitres (cL or cl). This is a metric unit of volume that is equal to one hundredth of a litre.

DEVELOP

Use your knowledge of volume and capacity to answer the following questions.

Volume

What is the volume of each of the following cubes and cuboids?

1. $3\,cm \times 7\,cm \times 5\,cm =$

2. $4\,cm \times 2\,cm \times 8\,cm =$

3. $6\,cm \times 6\,cm \times 6\,cm =$

4. $10\,cm \times 20\,cm \times 40\,cm =$

5. $0.5\,m \times 0.4\,m \times 0.6\,m =$

Capacity

Convert the following amounts into equivalent values.

6. How many millilitres in 1.3 litres?

7. Convert 2400 ml into litres.

8. What is 300 ml in centilitres?

9. How many lots of 25 ml will be needed to fill a 400 ml bottle?

10. How many millilitres in 9 centilitres?

A shape's volume is the measure of its total three-dimensional space.

TIMED TEST 18

① What is the volume of a cube that measures 4 m in height?

A	B	C	D	E
16 m³	32 m³	64 m³	24 m³	72 m³

② Find the missing measurement in this volume calculation. 9 cm × ? × 3 cm = 135 cm³

A	B	C	D	E
5 cm	3 cm	6 cm	7 cm	8 cm

③ The length of a cuboid is 21 cm and the width is 10 cm. If the volume is 4200 cm³, what is the height?

A	B	C	D	E
30 cm	40 cm	10 cm	20 cm	50 cm

④ What is the volume of a cuboid with these measurements?   L 6 cm   W 3.5 cm   H 3 cm

A	B	C	D	E
53 cm³	60 cm³	58 cm³	55 cm³	63 cm³

⑤ A small box has the following measurements: 5 cm length, 0.15 m width, 60 mm height. Work out the volume in millimetres cubed (mm³).

A	B	C	D	E
4500 mm³	450 000 mm³	4.5 mm³	200 mm³	300 mm³

⑥ If a bottle holds 2 litres and 300 ml are poured out, how much is left in the bottle?

A	B	C	D	E
700 ml	1700 ml	900 ml	1600 ml	2300 ml

⑦ A flask of tea holds 1 litre. If each cup holds approximately 200 ml, how many cups can be made from three flasks?

A	B	C	D	E
16	14	15	13	17

⑧ A full bottle holds 1.75 litres of lemonade. If three identical glasses holding 300 ml each are filled with lemonade, how much is left in the bottle in litres?

A	**B**	**C**	**D**	**E**
0.85 L	0.75 L	0.65 L	0.5 L	0.35 L

⑨ The width of a room is 5 m and its length is 10 m. What is the height if the total volume of the room is 100 m³?

A	**B**	**C**	**D**	**E**
10 m	20 m	2 m	2.5 m	10 m

⑩ A bath has a volume of 2.5 m³. What could be the dimensions of the bath?

A	**B**	**C**
2 m × 0.50 m × 0.5 m	1.5 m × 1 m × 1 m	1 m × 1.5 m × 2.5 m

D	**E**
3 m × 2 m × 1 m	1 m × 1 m × 2.5 m

⑪ What is the volume of this cuboid?

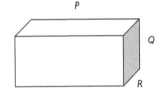

A	**B**	**C**	**D**	**E**
PQR	QR	P + Q + R	R + Q	PQ

⑫ The volume of the box below is 120 cm³.

What is the value of T?

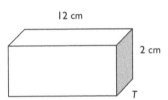

A	**B**	**C**	**D**	**E**
10 cm	8 cm	3 cm	2 cm	5 cm

⑬ If this cuboid has a volume of 450 cm³, what is the value of e?

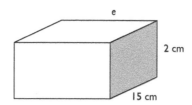

e

2 cm

15 cm

A

100 cm

B

250 cm

C

15 cm

D

10 cm

E

25 cm

⑭ If the volume of the cube is 8 cm³, what is the value of P?

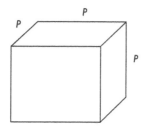

P

P

P

A

8 cm

B

2 cm

C

4 cm

D

6 cm

E

3 cm

⑮ If a swimming pool is 25 m long, 10 m wide and 2 m deep, how many litres of water can it hold? 1 cubic metre equals 1000 litres.

A

100 000 L

B

500 000 L

C

50 000 L

D

10 000 L

E

5000 L

**THIS PAGE HAS DELIBERATELY
BEEN LEFT BLANK**

SECTION 7:

GLOSSARY AND ANSWERS

Glossary

BIDMAS:	Stands for brackets, indices, division, multiplication, addition and subtraction, i.e. the order in which a calculation is carried out.
Brackets:	Symbols that show those terms that should be treated together and calculated first, in the order of operations.
Capacity:	The measure of the space within a 3D object.
Consecutive:	One number following the other continuously.
Continuous data:	Data that comes from measurement, such as weight.
Cube number:	A cube number is a number that has been produced by another number being multiplied by itself and by itself again, e.g. $3 \times 3 \times 3 = 27$. A cube number equals a whole number that has been raised to the power of 3.
Cumulative frequency:	A running sum of the frequencies.
Data:	Collective name for pieces of information, often used for reference or analysis.
Decimal place:	The position of a digit to the right of a decimal point.
Decimal point:	In a decimal number, the decimal point separates the whole number from the part that is smaller than 1.
Denominator:	The number at the bottom of a fraction, showing how many parts altogether.
Density:	The mass per unit volume of a solid.
Digit:	Any of the numerals from 0 to 9, especially when forming part of a number.
Discrete data:	Data that can be counted, such as number of house points collected in a week.
Equation:	Has an equals sign in it, e.g. $3x + 1 = 7$.
Estimate:	Roughly calculate or judge the value, number or quantity.
Exchange:	To 'borrow' in subtraction.
Expression:	A collection of terms or variables, e.g. $2x + 2y$ or $5r + 6$ without an equals sign.
Factor:	A number or quantity that when multiplied with another produces a given number or expression.
Formula:	A mathematical relationship or rule expressed in symbols. The plural is formulae.
Fraction:	A numerical quantity that is not a whole number.
Frequency:	The number of times an event occurs.
Frequency chart:	A table that shows the total for each category or group of data.
Imperial system:	A measuring system based on feet, gallons and pounds as units of length, capacity and weight or mass.
Index (power):	The index of a number shows how many times to use the number in multiplication. It is written as a small number to the right and above the base number. In this example: $4^3 = 4 \times 4 \times 4 = 64$. The plural of index is indices.

Integer:	A whole number.
Interval:	An interval is the distance between one number and the next on the scale of a graph.
Length:	The distance of the longest dimension of a shape.
Linear:	A straight line on a graph.
Line graph:	A graph formed by joining points together with straight lines.
Mass:	The weight of an object. A measure of how much matter is in an object. Mass is measured in grams and kilograms in the metric system and in pounds and stones in the imperial system.
Metric system:	The decimal measuring system based on the metre, litre and gram as units of length, capacity and weight or mass. Converted in powers of 10.
Multiples:	The numbers in multiplication tables, e.g. multiples of 3 are: 3, 6, 9, 12, etc.
Numerator:	The number above the line in a fraction, showing how many parts you have.
Place value:	The numerical value that a digit has by virtue of its position in a number.
Power:	The power of a number shows how many times to use the number in a multiplication. It is written as a small number to the right and above the base number.
Prime number:	A number that only has two factors: itself and 1.
Product:	The result when two numbers are multiplied together.
Quotient:	A result obtained by dividing one quantity by another.
Regroup:	Regrouping is often used in subtraction and addition. It is also known as 'carrying', 'exchanging' and 'borrowing' numbers.
Rounding:	Alteration of a number to one that is less exact but more convenient for calculations.
Sequence:	A set of numbers containing a pattern.
Significant figures:	Each of the digits of a number that are used to express it to the required degree of accuracy, starting from the first non-zero digit.
Square number:	A square number is a number that results from another number being multiplied by itself, e.g. $2 \times 2 = 4$. A square number equals a whole number that has been raised to the power of 2.
Substitution:	The act of replacing a letter with a number or a number with a letter.
Tabulate:	To put information into a table format.
Tally chart:	A table with tally marks to show a data set.
Term:	One of the parts of an expression or a number in a number sequence.
Triangular number:	A number that can be represented by a triangular pattern of dots.
Vertices:	A corner on a shape is referred to as a vertex. The plural is vertices.
Volume:	The amount of space that a substance or object occupies, or that is enclosed within a container.

Answers

Lesson 1: Place Value

Develop (page 9)

①

    A   600 million

    B   30 thousand

    C   700 or seven hundred

    D $\frac{5}{10}$ or five tenths

    E $\frac{6}{1000}$ or six thousandths

    F $\frac{1}{1\,000\,000}$ or one millionth

②   a)

        i)   3621.43

        ii)   728.91

    b)

        i)   462.38

        ii)   2.3941

Lesson 2: Rounding Numbers

Develop (page 11)

①

    a)   86 700

    b)   86 734.29

    c)   86 730

    d)   86 734.3

②

    a)   2864.4

    b)   3000

    c)   2900

③

    a)   867

    b)   867.43

    c)   867

Timed Test 1 (page 12)

Question	Answer
1.	D = 30 000
2.	B = 629 416.5782
3.	A = 3678.9
4.	E = two thousandths
5.	C = £29 450
6.	E = 130 000
7.	C = 23 420 ft
8.	A = 83.4 s
9.	C = 35 000
10.	D = 186 500
11.	A = 10 000
12.	B = 14 000
13.	E = 3 500 000 kg
14.	A = 605 005 027
15.	E = 1 h 27 m 32.5 s

Lesson 3: Special Numbers and Number Sequences

Develop (page 17)

① 81   100   121   (square numbers)

② 23   29   31   (prime numbers)

③ 100   81   64   (square numbers)

④ 8   64   216   (cube numbers)

⑤ 24   40   30   (alternate sequence)

⑥ 6   21   36   (triangular numbers)

⑦ 63   45   27   (9 times table)

⑧ 13   21   34   (Fibonacci sequence)

⑨ 159   319   639   (double the number and then add 1)

⑩ 240   60   15   (divide by 2 each time)

Lesson 4: Addition and Subtraction

Develop (page 21)

① 353.12

② 18.89

③ 1127.43

④ 21.33

⑤ 1013

⑥ 79.2

⑦ 6.993

⑧ 2978.002

⑨ £736.55

⑩ 1093.35

Timed Test 2 (page 22)

Question	Answer	Explanation
1.	C = 310	142 goals + 168 goals = 310 goals
2.	B = 2786 L	6000 L − 3214 L = 2786 L
3.	A = 12.55 m	9.75 m + 2.8 m = 12.55 m
4.	E = 341.69 cm	87.91 cm + 36.32 cm + 209.40 cm + 8.06 cm = 341.69 cm
5.	D = 2750 m	Convert 4 km and 1.25 km to 4000 m and 1250 m 4000 m − 1250 m = 2750 m
6.	A = 8.811 m	8.9 m − 0.089 m = 8.811 m
7.	B = 3.8 km	31.5 km + 6.9 km = 38.4 km 42.2 km − 38.4 km = 3.8 km
8.	E = 5.84 kg	2.5 kg + 1.75 kg + 2.25 kg = 6.5 kg − 0.66 kg = 5.84 kg
9.	E = 63.88 kg	62.5 kg + 60.32 kg + 80 kg + 83.3 kg = 286.12 kg 350 kg − 286.12 kg = 63.88 kg
10.	D = 29.5 km	7.7 km + 12.3 km + 9.5 km = 29.5 km
11.	C = 7.5 h	1 h (maths) + 1.5 h (gym) + 1.75 h (ice skating) + 3.25 h (athletics) = 7.5 h
12.	B = 9900 m	10 000 m − 100 m = 9900 m
13.	C = 163	201 − 38 = 163 photographs
14.	D = 94	A pentagon has 5 sides, a rectangle has 4 sides, all triangles have 3 sides, an octagon has 8 sides $= (5 \times 3) + (2 \times 4) + (2 \times 3) + (3 \times 3) + (7 \times 8)$ $= (15 + 8 + 6 + 9) + (7 \times 8)$ $= 38 + 56$ $= 94$ sides
15.	B = 105.4	12.4 miles + 43.9 miles + 0.6 miles + 28.8 miles + 19.7 miles = 105.4 miles

Lesson 5: Multiplication

Develop (page 29)

1. 600

2. 27 000

3. 4.8

4. 0.24 mm²

5. 56.8

6. 6923.2

7. 91.648

8. 55.61

9. £671.50

10. 238.52

Timed Test 3 (page 30)

Question	Answer	Explanation
1.	D = 1944	324 × 6 = 1944 oak trees
2.	A = 4004	286 × 14 = 4004 people
3.	B = £408.50	86 × £4.75 = £408.50
4.	E = 1488 mm	32 × 46.5 mm = 1488 mm
5.	A = 3358	146 × 23 = 3358 passengers
6.	C = 14 580	324 × 45 = 14 580 napkins
7.	D = 20 864	326 × 64 = 20 864 pages
8.	C = £1161	£21.50 × 3 × 18 = £1161
9.	B = £664.64	£0.67 × 32 × 31 = £664.64
10.	E = 5168	19 × 34 × 8 = 5168 words
11.	C = 27 864	43 × 216 × 3 = 27 864 stitches
12.	A = 72	(5 + 1) × (6 × 2) = 6 × 12 = 72 minutes
13.	D = 21 252	253 × 84 = 21 252 passengers
14.	A = £137.34	£1.09 × 42 L × 3 = £137.34
15.	B = £8250	(5 boxes × 6 year groups × 50 packets) × £5.50 = £8250

Lesson 6: Division

Develop (page 35)

① 35

② 2839

③ 30615

④ 3421

⑤ 231

⑥ 142

⑦ 234

⑧ 321

⑨ 480

⑩ 562

Timed Test 4 (page 36)

Question	Answer	Explanation
1.	B = 12p	96p ÷ 8 = 12p
2.	D = £0.25	600p ÷ 24 = 25p
3.	E = 36	1 packet = 15 rolls 540 ÷ 15 = 36 packets of ham
4.	D = 25	1 week = 16 merit marks 400 ÷ 16 = 25 weeks
5.	E = 15	255 ÷ 17 = 15 students
6.	A = 20	500 ÷ 24 = 20 complete sheets
7.	E = 25p	£3 ÷ 12 = 25p
8.	D = 34	578 ÷ 17 = 34 nails
9.	E = 5m	$24 \times \square = 120$ 120 ÷ 24 = 5m
10.	D = 28	700 seats ÷ 25 schools = 28 students per coach
11.	B = 12	A square-based pyramid has 5 vertices. 60 ÷ 5 = 12
12.	D = 95	285 ÷ 3 = 95 children
13.	A = 2341 km	98322 ÷ 42 = 2341 km
14.	D = 512	$\frac{8}{30}$ of 1920. Therefore 1920 ÷ 30 = 64 64 × 8 = 512 sheep
15.	C = 14	33 + 51 = 84 ÷ 3 = 28 28 ÷ 2 = 14 fish each per day on average

Lesson 7: Multiplying and Dividing by 10, 100 and 1000

Develop (page 40)

1. 73.4
2. 8920
3. 30
4. 0.8
5. 0.657
6. 0.005
7. 6.78
8. 0.0074
9. 2100
10. 800

Lesson 8: Order of Operations (BIDMAS)

Develop (page 42)

1. $3 \times 16 = 48$
2. $30 \div 2 + 3 = 18$
3. $20 \div 4 = 5$
4. $7 + 4 = 11$
5. $4 + 6 = 10$
6. $3 \times (25 - 16) = 3 \times 9 = 27$
7. $40 \div 8 = 5$
8. $12 \div 4 = 3$
9. $2 + (8 \times 1) \times 4 = 2 + 8 \times 4 = 2 + 32 = 34$
10. $4 \times 64 = 256$

Try

a) $4 - 2 + 8 = 10$ or $4 \div 2 + 8 = 10$
b) $5 + 4 \times 6 - 8 = 21$
c) $2 + 6 \div 3 \times 4 = 10$
d) $1 + (3 \times 8) \div 6 - 2 = 3$

Timed Test 5 (page 43)

Question	Answer	Explanation
1.	C = £23.52	$(14 \times 8) \times 0.21 = £23.52$
2.	A = 20	1 length = 15 seconds 5 mins = $5 \times 60 = 300$ seconds $300 \div 15 = 20$ lengths
3.	E = 6	$£24 \times 1 + (8 \times £12)$ $£120 \div £20 = 6$
4.	B = 240	$(5 \times 4) \times 12$ $= 20 \times 12 = 240$ claws
5.	D = 136 s	$(8 \times 60) + 23 = 503$ seconds for Venus $(6 \times 60) + 7 = 367$ seconds for Mars $503 - 367$ $= 136$ seconds
6.	E = 2.55 L	Convert all bottles to ml. 300 ml + 750 ml + 1500 ml = 2550 ml = 2.55 litres
7.	A = £5354	$£8.50 \times 3h \times 2$ evenings per week $\times (52$ weeks $\times 2$ years$) + £50$ $= £51 \times (104) + £50$ $= £5354$
8.	C = 332	(26 cabbages × 6 rows) + (8 lettuces × 18 rows) + 32 cauliflowers = 156 + 144 + 32 = 332 vegetables
9.	A = 80	8 bottles × 750 ml = 6000 ml. 8 pineapples makes 600 ml. So 10 times this number are needed to make 6000 ml
10.	E = 114 L	2280 L × 3 days = 6840 6840 ÷ 60 cows = 114 litres
11.	B = £14	£1.75 − £1.25 = 50p profit per toy 50p × 28 toys = £14.00
12.	C = 350	$\frac{8}{8} - \frac{3}{8} = \frac{5}{8}$ of the children attended school 560 ÷ 8 = 70 70 × 5 = 350 children
13.	B = 25 920	4 supermarkets × (36 crates × 180 jars) = 4 × 6480 = 25 920 jars
14.	A = 8	23 pages × 12 cards = 276 cards 284 − 276 = 8 cards
15.	D = £110	£26 × 12 = £312 for total cost of lessons £85 + £117 = £202 currently saved £312 − £202 = £110 more to be saved

Lesson 9: Fractions

Develop (page 47)

① 36

② 36

③ 88

④ 60

⑤ 42

⑥ 27

⑦ 120

⑧ 800

⑨ 2280

⑩ 2160

Timed Test 6 (page 48)

Question	Answer	Explanation
1.	D = 80	$\frac{5}{25}$ of 100 = 20 golf balls. 100 − 20 = 80 golf balls
2.	E = £4.90	$\frac{6}{7}$ is equal to £4.20. So $\frac{1}{7}$ is 70 p. Adding £4.20 to 70 p gives £4.90
3.	A = $\frac{2}{5}$	Jack travels a total of 1200 m to school there and back. 3 km is equivalent to 3000 m. So $\frac{1200}{3000}$ can be simplified to $\frac{2}{5}$
4.	D = $\frac{2}{7}$	On a Tuesday and Wednesday, the baby would sleep 16 hours. The total for the week is 56 hours. $\frac{16}{56}$ in its lowest terms is $\frac{2}{7}$
5.	D = $\frac{1}{5}$	5 litres is equivalent to 5000 ml. The total amount in 4 bottles is 1000 ml (4 × 250 ml). $\frac{1000}{5000}$ can be simplified to $\frac{1}{5}$
6.	B = $\frac{1}{5}$	The total number of animals on Bracken Farm is 95. There are 19 ducks and this is one fifth of the total $\left(\frac{1}{5}\right)$
7.	B = $\frac{1}{8}$	Nigel spends 3 hours on the train every week day. 3 hours out of every 24 hours (full day) equates to $\frac{1}{8}$
8.	B = 20	There are 18 thirds in 6. Add 18 to two thirds $\left(\frac{2}{3}\right)$ and this equates to 20 thirds
9.	A = $\frac{5}{8}$	Brian has $\frac{3}{4}$ kg of liquorice which is equivalent to $\frac{6}{8}$. If he gives $\frac{1}{8}$ away this leaves $\frac{5}{8}$
10.	C = £12	Jason spends $\frac{1}{3}$ of £45 on clothes which is £15. $\frac{2}{5}$ on stationery which is £18. £18 + £15 = £33. This is subtracted from £45 to leave £12
11.	E = 48 miles	$\frac{3}{5}$ of 120 = 72, so Anita has already driven 72 miles. 120 subtract 72 leaves 48 miles left to drive
12.	C = 360 h	The farmer grows swedes on $\frac{4}{16}$ of 480 hectares which is 120 hectares. To find the hectares for the wheat the calculation is 480 − 120 = 360 hectares
13.	A = 525	She checks a total of $\frac{5}{12}$ on days 1 and 2. $\frac{5}{12}$ of 900 components is 375. To find the amount left, 900 subtract 375 equals 525
14.	B = £60	To find $\frac{6}{16}$ it is easier to simplify this fraction to $\frac{3}{8}$. $\frac{1}{8}$ equals £20. So to find $\frac{3}{8}$, multiply £20 by 3 to give £60
15.	C = $\frac{4}{25}$	$\frac{80}{500}$ voted other, and this can be simplified to $\frac{4}{25}$

Lesson 10: Decimals

Develop (page 51)

① 5.91

② 14.62

③ 1.44

④ 9.1

⑤ 7.59

⑥ 20

⑦ 1.05

⑧ 135.88

⑨ 20.25

⑩ 14.08

Timed Test 7 (page 52)

Question	Answer	Explanation
1.	E = 2.25	If you remove the decimal point it is 15 × 15 which is 225. Add the decimal point and it becomes 2.25
2.	C = 0.18	To find the difference use the inverse operation. Add 0.08 to 0.02 to make 0.1 and then add 0.1. Therefore, 0.08 + 0.1 = 0.18
3.	B = 11.8	To find the difference between the numbers round 38.2 to 40. This is 1.8. Then add 10 to 40. Therefore, 1.8 + 10 = 11.8
4.	B = 3.33	When the numbers are reordered, the middle (median) number is 3.33
5.	A = 99.01	93.41 + 5.6 = 99.01
6.	D = 5	You can say 'how many 1.2s in 6?' This question can be solved using repeated addition. 1.2 + 1.2 + 1.2 + 1.2 + 1.2 = 6 therefore $\frac{6}{1.2}$ = 5
7.	A = £10	If the pence amounts are added together, they equal £1. The pounds total £9. So £1 + £9 = £10
8.	B = 3.32 m	Convert 152 cm into metres, which is 1.52 m. Add together 1.45 m + 1.52 m + 0.35 m = 3.32 m
9.	E = 7.9 m	To find the mean, add together all the distances and divide by how many there are. 7.70 + 7.99 + 8.01 = $\frac{23.70}{3}$ = 7.9
10.	B = 11.1	Counting back 15 tenths is equivalent to subtracting 1.5. 12.6 − 1.5 = 11.1
11.	B = 14	Use the inverse operation, 0.5 × ? = 7
12.	C = 5	Use repeated addition or multiplication. 330 ml × 5 = 1.650 L
13.	B = £27.44	Convert all the amounts into the same value, either pounds or pence, i.e. £0.88 + £8 + £0.80 + £8.08 + £8.88 + £0.80
14.	A = 3 L	Convert 100 cl to 1 litre and add all the numbers together. 1.2 + 1.0 + 0.8 = 3.0
15.	D = 1.331	If you remove the decimal point it becomes 11 × 11 × 11 = 1331 Put the decimal point back in and it becomes 1.331

Lesson 11: Percentages

Develop (page 55)

①	8	⑥	2100
②	9	⑦	15
③	24	⑧	54
④	70	⑨	34.5
⑤	750	⑩	368

Timed Test 8 (page 56)

Question	Answer	Explanation
1.	B = 196	2% of 200 is 4. 200 − 4 = 196
2.	C = 70%	There are 420 fiction books (600 − 180). $\frac{420}{600}$ is equivalent to $\frac{7}{10}$. This is 70%
3.	D = £144	20% of £120 = £24. £120 + £24 = £144
4.	B = 75%	$\frac{60}{80}$ is equivalent to $\frac{3}{4}$. $\frac{3}{4}$ = 75%
5.	A = £120	25% is the same as $\frac{1}{4}$. $\frac{1}{4}$ of £160 is £40. £160 − £40 = £120
6.	E = £345	15% of £300 is £45. £300 + £45 = £345
7.	B = £5082	21% of £4200 = £882. £4200 + £882 = £5082
8.	C = 240	25% of 320 = 80 beds. 320 − 80 = 240
9.	B = £1872	4% of £1800 = £72. £1800 + £72 = £1872
10.	B = £1045	5% of £1100 = £55. £1100 − £55 = £1045
11.	E = £280	8% of £3500 = £280
12.	C = 10%	£7.92 − £7.20 = £0.72. $\frac{72}{720}$ is equivalent to 10%
13.	A = £4.95	10% of £4.50 = 45 p. £4.50 + 45 p = £4.95
14.	B = 279	7% of 300 = 21. 300 − 21 = 279
15.	C = 80%	450 000 − 250 000 = 200 000. 200 000 ÷ 250 000 × 100 = 80

Lesson 12: The *n*th Term

Develop (page 61)

① **D** $3n - 1$

② **C** $(n + 2)^2$

③ **D** $n^2 - 3$

④ 3 $4 \div 2 + 1$

⑤ 38 $4 \times 10 - 2$

⑥ 20 $5^2 - 5$

⑦ 198 99×2

⑧ 57 $4 \times 15 - 3$

⑨ 10th term $10^2 = 100$

⑩ Yes $6 \times 3 = 18 - 4 = 14$

Lesson 13: Introduction to Algebra

Develop (page 63)

① $M = 2$

② $t = 7$

③ $w = 9$

④ $y = 21$

⑤ $H = 45$

⑥ $5 + 6 = 11$

⑦ $3 \times 6 = 18$

⑧ $5 \times 6 \div 3 = 10$

⑨ $5 + 2 \times 6 + 10 = 27$

⑩ $6 \times 10 - 5 = 55$

⑪ $2d$

⑫ $3c$

⑬ $2k$

⑭ 16

⑮ 3

Lesson 14: Solving Algebraic Equations

Develop (page 67)

① $y = 6$ $2y = 12$ $y = 12 ÷ 2$

② $R = 8$ $5R = 40$ $R = 40 ÷ 5$

③ $n = 3$ $14n = 22 + 20$ $14n = 42$ $n = 42 ÷ 14$

④ $M = 5$ $41 - 6 = 7M$ $35 ÷ 7$

⑤ $W = 4$ $16W = 73 - 9$ $16W = 64$

⑥ $R = 32$ $R ÷ 8 = 10 - 6$ $R ÷ 8 = 4$ $R = 4 × 8$

⑦ $J = 56$ $J ÷ 7 = 3 + 5$ $J ÷ 7 = 8$ $J = 7 × 8$

⑧ $T = 96$ $T ÷ 24 = 32 - 28$ $T ÷ 24 = 4$ $T = 4 × 24$

⑨ $y = 2$ $7y - y = 1 + 11$ $6y = 12$ $y = 12 ÷ 6$

⑩ $x = 1$ $17x - 9x = 2 + 6$ $8x = 8$

Timed Test 9 (page 68)

Question	Answer	Explanation
1.	D = 126	$5^3 + 1 = 126$ ($5 × 5 × 5 = 125$)
2.	A = 57	$4 × 15 - 3$
3.	E = 54	$(8 + 10)3 = 18 × 3 = 54$
4.	C = 4e	$6 × e - 2 × e = 6e - 2e = 4e$
5.	D = 3g + 2h	$g + g + 2 × h + g = 2g + 2h + g = 3g + 2h$
6.	C = 100	$A ÷ 10 - 5 = 5$ $A ÷ 10 = 5 + 5$ $A ÷ 10 = 10$, so $A = 100$
7.	B = 100	$x ÷ 2 - 16 = 34$ $x = (34 + 16) × 2 = 100$
8.	D = £6.50	£4.20 + £2.30
9.	A = 29	$12 + (16 - 2) + B + 1 = 56$ $27 + B = 56$ $B = 56 - 27 = 29$
10.	E = 3	$22 - (6 + 4 + 2 + 5 + 2) = 22 - 19 = 3$
11.	C = £32	$4F + £60 + £7 = £195$ $£195 - £7 - £60 = 128 ÷ 4 = £32$
12.	B = 44	$22 + (8 × 2) + 6 = 44$
13.	A = 9	$15 - 6 = 9$
14.	C = 20	$50 ÷ 2.5 = 20$
15.	E = 13	$(50 - 11) ÷ 3 = 13$

Lesson 15: Ratio and Proportion

Develop (page 74)

①	3 : 5	③	7 : 2	⑤	10 : 3	⑦	4 : 1	⑨	9 : 7
②	6 : 4	④	1 : 250	⑥	3 : 1	⑧	8 : 7	⑩	1 : 4

Timed Test 10 (page 75)

Question	Answer	Explanation
1.	B = 80 p	3 + 2 + 1 = 6 'equal parts'. Divide £2.40 by 6 to work out one part of the ratio = £0.40. Daisy had a ratio of 2. 2 × £0.40 = 80 p
2.	D = 30	5 + 3 + 1 = 9 'equal parts'. Divide 54 sweets by 9 to work out one part of the ratio = 6. Arzaan had a ratio of 5. 5 × 6 = 30
3.	C = £600	2 + 3 = 5 'equal parts'. Divide £1000 by 5 to work out one part of the ratio = £200. Kushi had a ratio of 3. 3 × £200 = £600
4.	E = 63	7 + 3 = 10 'equal parts'. Divide 90 beads by 10 to work out one part of the ratio = 9. Silver has a ratio of 7. 7 × 9 = 63
5.	A = 500 000 m	1 cm = 100 km. 5 × 100 km = 500 km. Multiply 500 km by 1000 to convert into metres = 500 000 m
6.	D = 8	4 + 2 + 1 = 7 'equal parts'. Divide 14 orange segments by 7 to work out one part of the ratio = 2. The largest share has a ratio of 4, therefore 4 × 2 = 8
7.	B = 8	7 + 4 + 2 = 13 'equal parts'. Divide 52 playing cards by 13 to work out one part of the ratio = 4. The smallest share has a ratio of 2, therefore 4 × 2 = 8
8.	C = 36	2 + 3 + 1 = 6 'equal parts'. Divide 108 biscuits by 6 to work out one part of the ratio = 18. Two parts of the ratio is 18 × 2 = 36
9.	E = 240	3 + 2 + 2 = 7 'equal parts'. Divide 560 runs by 7 to work out one part of the ratio = 80. Freddie had a ratio of 3, therefore 80 × 3 = 240
10.	B = 20	1 + 4 + 2 + 1 + 3 = 11 'equal parts'. Divide 55 cars by 11 to work out one part of the ratio = 5. The ratio for red cars was 4, therefore 4 × 5 = 20
11.	C = 1.5 m	1 cm = 30 cm of the model train. 5 cm × 30 cm = 150 cm. To convert into metres, divide by 100. 150 ÷ 100 = 1.5 m
12.	A = 48	1 + 2 + 3 + 4 + 1 + 1 = 12 'equal parts'. Divide 144 sweets by 12 to work out one part of the ratio = 12. The greatest proportion of sweets was a ratio of 4, therefore 4 × 12 = 48
13.	D = 67.5 km	1 cm = 9 km on the map. 7.5 × 9 = 67.5 km
14.	B = 150 L	3 + 5 = 8 'equal parts'. Divide 240 litres by 8 to work out one part of the ratio = 30 L. 5 parts of water was added, therefore 30 L × 5 = 150 L
15.	D = 30	70 − 10 (for Kajol) = 60, $\frac{1}{3}$ of 60 = 20 (for Rajan). 6 + 2 = 8 'equal parts'. Divide the remaining 40 sweets by 8 to work out one part of the ratio = 5 sweets. Dad gets 6 parts, 5 × 6 = 30 sweets

Lesson 16: Probability

Develop (page 78)

①	$\frac{1}{2}$	③	$\frac{1}{8}$	⑤	$\frac{3}{10}$	⑦	$\frac{1}{12}$	⑨	$\frac{3}{4}$
②	$\frac{1}{4}$	④	$\frac{1}{7}$	⑥	$\frac{5}{12}$	⑧	$\frac{1}{2}$	⑩	$\frac{11}{12}$

Timed Test 11 (page 79)

Question	Answer	Explanation
1.	$D = \frac{3}{4}$	There are 8 balls altogether (5 + 2 + 1). Add the red and white balls together, 1 + 5 = 6. Therefore 6 out of 8 = $\frac{3}{4}$
2.	$C = \frac{4}{7}$	There are now 7 balls altogether after a white ball has been removed (4 + 2 + 1). The chance of picking a white ball is $\frac{4}{7}$
3.	$A = \frac{1}{13}$	There are 4 aces in a pack of cards. $\frac{4}{52}$ in its simplest form is $\frac{1}{13}$
4.	$D = \frac{12}{52}$	Altogether there are 12 picture cards (3 pictures × 4 suits). As a probability it is $\frac{12}{52}$
5.	$C = \frac{1}{52}$	There is only 1 King of Diamonds, so it has only 1 chance of being selected from the 52 cards
6.	$B = \frac{1}{3}$	There are 3 slow songs and 2 house tunes, so 5 songs combined. $\frac{5}{15}$ can be simplified to $\frac{1}{3}$
7.	$E = \frac{11}{15}$	15 songs altogether minus 4 hip-hop songs is $\frac{11}{15}$
8.	$D = \frac{1}{18}$	There are 36 pencils altogether (5 + 2 + 8 + 15 + 6) with 2 blue pencils. $\frac{2}{36}$ can be simplified to $\frac{1}{18}$. The information about the new box is redundant.
9.	$B = \frac{7}{36}$	The total of red and blue pencils is 7 (2 + 5) and there are 36 pencils in total
10.	$E = \frac{3}{13}$	As 10 black pencils have been lost there are now 26 pencils (36 − 10). The probability of choosing a green pencil is $\frac{6}{26}$ which can be simplified to $\frac{3}{13}$
11.	$A = 50$	The defective rate of calculators is $\frac{1}{20}$. Divide 1000 calculators by 20, which is 50
12.	$C = $ certain	It is certain to be a green ball as there is only 1 yellow ball which has already been taken out
13.	$D = \frac{5}{6}$	36 chocolates minus 6 milk chocolates leaves 30 dark chocolates. $\frac{30}{36}$ simplified is $\frac{5}{6}$
14.	$A = \frac{3}{8}$	There are 8 possible outcomes (HHH, HTH, HHT, HTT, THH, TTH, THT, TTT) so the probability of two coins landing heads up is $\frac{3}{8}$
15.	$B = \frac{1}{1296}$	There are a possible 1296 outcomes (6 × 6 × 6 × 6). Therefore the probability of throwing 4 ones is $\frac{1}{1296}$

Lesson 17: Averages

Develop (page 82)

①   20

②   15

③   12

④   15.5

Timed Test 12 (page 83)

Question	Answer	Explanation
1.	E = 5 km	The total distance covered was 30 km and Ankush recorded 6 running journeys, therefore 30 ÷ 6 = 5 km
2.	D = 400 ml	The total is 2000 ml, therefore 2000 divided by 5 gives 400 ml
3.	A = 6 kg	The total mass of John's pets is 36 kg and he has 6 pets, therefore 36 ÷ 6 = 6 kg
4.	E = 17	When the coat sales are reordered 12, 14, 17, 32, 47, the middle number is 17
5.	C = £3.50	The range is the difference between £4.75 and £1.25, which equals £3.50
6.	C = 52 minutes	The total length of time of the programmes is 260 minutes. Therefore 260 divided by 5 is 52 minutes
7.	A = £3	The total cost of the biscuits is £15 and if this amount is divided by 5 it gives £3
8.	D = 1010 ft	If you reorder these values from the smallest to the largest, the middle value is 1010 ft
9.	C = 30 000	The total number of tickets sold was 150 000 and if this is divided by 5 performances it gives a mean of 30 000
10.	B = 28°C	To work out the range, find the difference between the highest and lowest temperatures, 21°C and −7°C, to get 28°C
11.	C = 90 kg	To work out the mean mass, divide 630 kg by 7, which equals 90 kg
12.	B = 5.5	If you reorder these values from the smallest to the largest, the middle value is 5.5
13.	D = 283	To work out the mean, you need to add up all the numbers, 227 + 103 + 258 + 386 + 441 = 1415. Divide the total by 5. 1415 ÷ 5 = 283
14.	A = £5.31	To work out the range, find the highest amount, £6.70, and take away the lowest amount, £1.39, to give the answer £5.31
15.	D = 195	Multiply 5 by 180 = 900. Now take away the numbers you already have from 900. 900 − 155 − 162 − 190 − 198 = 195. The fifth number is 195

Lesson 18: Conversion

Develop (page 87)

Metric conversion

1. 38400 cm
2. 9.8 kg
3. 27.3 L
4. 800 cm
5. 980 mm
6. 9700 m
7. 700 ml
8. 70 g
9. 42 cm
10. 7000 mm

Time conversion

11. 108 months
12. 1800 years
13. 24 minutes
14. 120 years
15. 7000 years
16. 420 minutes
17. 36000 seconds
18. 744 hours
19. 12600 seconds
20. 2922 (includes two leap years)

Timed Test 13 (page 88)

Question	Answer	Explanation
1.	B = 120	$6 \times 1000 = 6000 \div 50$ ml = 120
2.	E = 5040 mins	$7 \times 3 \times 4 \times 60 = 5040$. $21 \times 4 = 84$. $84 \times 60 = 5040$
3.	A = 10.5 km	$3.5 \times 3000 = 10500$ m. 10500 m $\div 1000 = 10.5$ km
4.	C = 219 144 h	6×366 (leap years every 4 years) $\times 24 = 52704$ $19 \times 365 \times 24 = 166440$ $52704 + 166440 = 219144$ hours
5.	E = 4.8 km	4 metres = 1 s $\times 60 = 240$ m in 1 min. 240 m $\times 20 = 4800$ m in 20 mins
6.	A = 5040 mins	$3.5 \times 24 = 84$ hours. $84 \times 60 = 5040$ minutes
7.	B = 1500 g	1 box = 10 tins = 15 kg. $15000 \div 10 = 1500$ g
8.	C = 6.7 km	240000 cm $\div 100$ to get to metres = 2400 m run 800 m swim 3.5 km = 3500 m cycle 6700 m: to convert to km $\div 1000 = 6.7$ km
9.	A = 0.4 kg	4×1.5 kg = 6 kg = 6000 g $\div 15 = 400$ g = 0.4 kg
10.	B = 4750 ml	4.75 L $\times 1000 = 4750$
11.	C = 1500	25 mins $\times 60 = 1500$ s
12.	D = 68000 g	$17 \times 4 \times 1000 = 68000$ g
13.	B = 214.76 m	1 yd = 0.91 m. $0.91 \times 236 = 214.76$
14.	D = £72.90	1 gallon = 4.5 litres. 15 gallons = 67.5 litres. 67.5 litres $\times$ £1.08 = £72.90
15.	E = 6	1 acre = $\frac{2}{5}$ hectare $15 \div 5 = 3$. $3 \times 2 = 6$ 15 acres = 6 hectares

Lesson 19: Bar Charts

Develop (page 96)

① 104

② 30 shops

③ Town 3

④ 15 shops

⑤ 46 shops

Lesson 20: Line Graphs

Develop (page 99)

① Friday

② Monday and Sunday

③ Tuesday

④ 42.5 hours

⑤ 6 hours

Lesson 21: Pie Charts, Pictograms and Venn Diagrams

Develop (page 101)

① 180 children

② 40%

③ 36°

④ 252 children

⑤ 120 children

⑥ 160 children

⑦ 70 children

⑧ 230 children

⑨ Sport

⑩ 130

⑪ 4 children

⑫ 1 child

⑬ 5 children

⑭ 30 children

⑮ 10 children

Timed Test 14 (page 103)

Question	Answer	Explanation
1.	C = Aug	August is the warmest month at 32 degrees
2.	A = Jun & Jul	Both June and July have the same temperatures in northern France at 25 degrees
3.	B = Jan	January had the lowest recorded temperature at 3 degrees
4.	E = 27 degrees	The range of temperature in southern France is 5 to 32 degrees
5.	B = £5	5 euros converts to £5 on the chart
6.	A = 6 euros	£6 converts to 6 euros on the chart
7.	A = £15	We can see that 5 euros equals £5. There are three lots of 5 euros in 15 euros. Then multiply £5 by 3 to give the answer £15
8.	D = 60°	The pie chart is divided into 12 sectors. 360° divided by 12 is 30, so each sector is 30°. Two sectors are blue representing dance and so the total angle for dance is 30° + 30°
9.	E = 420	Add together the number of children who like computer games (3 sectors) and football (4 sectors). 7 sectors = 7 × 60 = 420 children
10.	D = $\frac{1}{6}$	2 sectors represent dance: this equates to $\frac{2}{12}$. $\frac{1}{6}$ is its simplest form
11.	B = 25%	3 sectors represent computer games. This equates to $\frac{3}{12}$ which is $\frac{1}{4}$ or 25%
12.	E = 450	The chart shows 4 and a half bottles. Each bottle equates to 100 that were collected. 4 × 100 = 400. 400 + ($\frac{100}{2}$) = 450
13.	A = 150	425 crisp packets were collected (4 and a quarter packets are in the chart) and 275 cans were collected (2 and $\frac{3}{4}$ cans are in the chart). The difference is 425 − 275 = 150
14.	C = 700	425 crisp packets were collected (4 and a quarter packets are in the chart) and 275 cans were collected (2 and $\frac{3}{4}$ cans are in the chart). In total 700 items were collected (425 crisp packets + 275 cans)
15.	B = 1150	425 crisp packets + 275 cans + 450 bottles = 1150 in total

Lesson 22: Angles

Develop (page 110)

① reflex angle

② 90° and it is called a right angle

③ acute angle

④ 540°

⑤ obtuse angle

⑥ 163°

⑦ 50°

⑧ 69°

⑨ 60°

⑩ A = 96°, B = 84°

Timed Test 15 (page 111)

Question	Answer	Explanation
1.	A = 31°	Angles on a straight line add up to 180°. Therefore 130° + 19° = 149°, 180° − 149° = 31°
2.	E = north west	Turning 270° is the same as three 90° turns. It is important to turn anti-clockwise. The ship will be facing north west
3.	B = 135°	The interior angles in a regular octagon total 1080 ((n − 2) × 180 = 1080). There are 8 angles, therefore 1080 ÷ 8 = 135°
4.	D = east	Turning 135° is the same as 90° + 45° turns. Zak will be facing east
5.	E = 92°	The degrees inside a triangle total 180°, therefore 67° + 21° = 88°, 180 − 88° = 92°
6.	D = 10	The formula for working out interior angles is ((n − 2) × 180 = total interior angles). Therefore, if 10 was the number of sides (10 − 2) × 180 = 1440°
7.	C = 120°	Between each number in a clock face there are 30°. There are 4 equal spaces between 10 o'clock and 2 o'clock moving clockwise, therefore 30 × 4 = 120°
8.	C = 70°	Both angles at the base of an isosceles triangle are the same. Take away the angle you know: 180° − 40° = 140°. 140° ÷ 2 = 70°
9.	E = 135°	The degrees inside a pentagon sum to 540° ((n sides − 2) × 180). If you subtract 115°, 90°, 90° and 110°, this leaves 135°
10.	B = 69°	The straight line totals 180°. A 90° angle is shown plus 21°, equalling 111°. Therefore 180° − 111° = 69°
11.	C = 202°	A reflex angle is greater than 180° therefore 202° is the only option
12.	B = 145°	A supplementary angle equals 180°. So, if 180° − 35° = 145°, 145° is the supplementary angle
13.	D = 35°	A complementary angle totals 90°. Therefore 90° − 55° = 35°
14.	E = 112°	The interior angles of all quadrilaterals total 360°. The given angles total 248° (95° + 95° + 58°). 360° − 248° = 112°
15.	B = 216°	A trapezium has four sides. So 72° + 72° = 144°. 360° − 144° = 216°

Lesson 23: 2D Shapes
Develop (page 114)

1. 1
2. 4
3. Examples: square, rectangle, kite, trapezium, parallelogram
4. heptagon
5. B
6. 2
7. 4
8. 10
9. nonagon
10. irregular heptagon

Lesson 24: 3D Shapes
Develop (page 116)

1. 6
2. 3
3. 24
4. 4
5. 15
6. $(8 \times 0) = 0$
7. 2
8. 12
9. 8
10. cylinder

Timed Test 16 (page 118)

Question	Answer	Explanation
1.	A	Parallel lines do not touch or cross over, therefore B, C and D are ruled out
2.	C = 19	A nonagon has 9 sides and a decagon has 10 sides. 10 + 9 = 19
3.	B = scalene	If the angles are all different the triangle is called scalene
4.	B = 4	The order of rotation is 4 because this shape can rotate exactly 4 times on itself
5.		A **rectangle** has **two** pairs of equal **sides**. The angles are all **equal** and the **diagonals** are equal. Each angle is **ninety** degrees. This shape is sometimes called an oblong. It has two pairs of **parallel** sides.
6.	C = 56	A heptagon has seven vertices and an octagon has eight sides. 7 × 8 = 56
7.	C	All quadrilaterals have four sides. A trapezium is a four-sided shape
8.	D = 3	A nonagon is a nine-sided shape and a scalene triangle has three sides. 9 ÷ 3 = 3
9.	D	The octagon has eight sides
10.	B	Perpendicular lines create a right angle. Therefore, the only option is B
11.	A = 14	A cuboid has six faces and eight vertices. 6 + 8 = 14
12.	D = 12	A hexagonal prism has six corners at each end. 6 + 6 = 12
13.	B = 10	A cone has two faces and a triangular prism has five. 5 × 2 = 10
14.	D = square-based pyramid	The net when folded will create a square-based pyramid
15.	C = 12	There are two hemispheres in a sphere. Therefore, 2 × 6 = 12

Lesson 25: Perimeter and Area

Develop (page 121)

①   16 m

②   81 cm²

③   7 cm

④   90 cm²

⑤   48 cm

⑥   13 m

⑦ $\frac{1}{2}(Q \times P)\,m^2$

⑧   8 cm

⑨   25 cm

⑩   3 cm

Timed Test 17 (page 123)

Question	Answer	Explanation
1.	D = 36 cm²	The perimeter is 24 cm, therefore each side is 6 cm (24 ÷ 4 = 6). To find the area, multiply the length by the width, 6 × 6 = 36 cm²
2.	A = 6 cm	The area is 60 cm². The length is 10 cm, so 60 cm² ÷ 10 cm = 6 cm. The width is 6 cm
3.	B = 36 cm	The perimeter is 2(L + W), therefore 2 × (7 + 11) = 36 cm
4.	D = 144 m²	The area is L × W, therefore 12 m × 12 m = 144 m²
5.	D = 63 cm	A heptagon has 7 sides. Each side is 9 cm. To find the perimeter multiply 7 × 9 = 63 cm
6.	C = w + w + w	To find the perimeter of the triangle, you must add together the three sides. Therefore, w + w + w equals the perimeter
7.	C = $(\frac{1}{2}R)Q$	The area of the isosceles triangle is calculated by $\frac{1}{2}$ base × height therefore $(\frac{1}{2}R) \times Q$
8.	B = 32 cm²	w = 4 cm. Area = length × width. 4 cm × 8 cm = 32 cm²
9.	C = 20 cm	Area = length × width, so 100 ÷ 5 = 20. l = 20 cm
10.	E = 10 cm	The area of the rectangle would be 50 cm². This would be halved for the triangle to be 25 cm². Therefore, the length is 10 cm as 10 × 5 = 50 cm²
11.	D = 360 cm	To find the perimeter in metres, add together (0.6 + 1.2) × 2 = 3.6 m. To convert metres to centimetres, multiply by 100. 3.6 × 100 = 360 cm
12.	E = 8 m	Both lengths total 16 m. 24 m − 16 m = 8 m. The two widths together total 8 m
13.	D = 2100 mm²	The tag has an area of 6 cm × 3.5 cm = 60 mm × 35 mm = 2100 mm²
14.	B = 0.2 m²	To find the area of a parallelogram, multiply the base by the height. 0.5 m × 0.4 m = 0.2 m²
15.	D = 7	To find the area, multiply L × W. 8 m × 12.5 m = 100 m². One bag covers 16 m². So 100 ÷ 16 = 6.25. Therefore 7 bags are needed

Lesson 26: Volume and Capacity

Develop (page 126)

① 105 cm³
② 64 cm³
③ 216 cm³
④ 8000 cm³
⑤ 0.12 m³
⑥ 1300 ml
⑦ 2.4 L
⑧ 30 cl
⑨ 16
⑩ 90 ml

Timed Test 18 (page 127)

Question	Answer	Explanation
1.	C = 64 m³	Volume is L × W × H, so a cube of 4 m × 4 m × 4 m equals 64 m³
2.	A = 5 cm	To find the missing number, multiply the two measurements you have and then divide this into the total volume. 9 cm × 3 cm = 27 cm². 135 cm³ divided by 27 cm² = 5 cm
3.	D = 20 cm	To find the missing number, multiply the two measurements you have and then divide this into the total volume. 21 cm × 10 cm = 210 cm². 4200 cm³ divided by 210 cm² = 20 cm
4.	E = 63 cm³	Volume is L × W × H, therefore 6 × 3.5 × 3 equals 63 cm³
5.	B = 450 000 mm³	First convert all measurements to millimetres, therefore 50 mm × 150 mm × 60 mm = 450 000 mm³
6.	B = 1700 ml	Convert all measurements to millilitres before attempting the question. 2000 ml − 300 ml = 1700 ml
7.	C = 15	Three flasks equate to 3000 ml (3 × 1000 ml) 3000 ml ÷ 200 ml = 15
8.	A = 0.85 L	Three glasses of lemonade equals 0.9 L (300 ml × 3). Subtracting 0.9 L from 1.75 L equals 0.85 L
9.	C = 2 m	To find the missing number, multiply the two measurements you have and then divide this into the total volume. 5 m × 10 m = 50 m². 100 m³ divided by 50 m² = 2 m
10.	E = 1 m × 1 m × 2.5 m	1 m × 1 m × 2.5 m = 2.5 m³
11.	A = PQR	Volume is L × W × H, therefore P × Q × R is the same as PQR
12.	E = 5 cm	To find the missing number, multiply the two measurements you have and then divide this into the total volume. 12 cm × 2 cm = 24 cm². 120 cm³ divided by 24 cm² = 5 cm
13.	C = 15 cm	Divide 450 cm³ by (15 cm × 2 cm) = 15 cm
14.	B = 2 cm	2 cm × 2 cm × 2 cm = 8 cm³. P = 2 cm
15.	B = 500 000 L	25 m × 10 m × 2 m = 500 m³. Therefore 500 × 1000 L = 500 000 L

**THIS PAGE HAS DELIBERATELY
BEEN LEFT BLANK**

Marking Chart

Fill in the tables below with your results from each of the Timed Tests. Each test is marked out of 15.

Colour the Progress Grid on pages 158 and 159 to see how well you have done.

	Timed Test 1	Timed Test 2	Timed Test 3
Score	/15	/15	/15

	Timed Test 4	Timed Test 5	Timed Test 6
Score	/15	/15	/15

	Timed Test 7	Timed Test 8	Timed Test 9
Score	/15	/15	/15

	Timed Test 10	Timed Test 11	Timed Test 12
Score	/15	/15	/15

	Timed Test 13	Timed Test 14	Timed Test 15
Score	/15	/15	/15

	Timed Test 16	Timed Test 17	Timed Test 18
Score	/15	/15	/15

Progress Grid

Colour the grids below with your total mark from each Timed Test to see how well you have done.

Timed Test 1

Timed Test 2

Timed Test 3

Timed Test 4

Timed Test 5

Timed Test 6

Timed Test 7

Timed Test 8

Timed Test 9

Timed Test 10

Timed Test 11

Timed Test 12

Timed Test 13

Timed Test 14

Timed Test 15

Timed Test 16

Timed Test 17

Timed Test 18

Read the statements below for some hints and tips.

0–7: Carefully re-read the 'Learn' section and try the 'Develop' questions again. When you feel confident, retry the Timed Test.

8–12: Good effort, make sure you learn from your mistakes. Review the answers of the questions that you have got wrong and understand the correct calculations for next time.

13–15: Well done, you have shown a secure understanding!

THIS PAGE HAS DELIBERATELY
BEEN LEFT BLANK